Modern Chinese Cultural Encounters

Volume I
Studying and Traveling in China

Judy Zhu

iUniverse, Inc.
New York   Bloomington

Modern Chinese Cultural Encounters
Volume I Studying and Traveling in China

*The views expressed in this work are solely those of the author and do not
necessarily reflect the views of the publisher, and the publisher hereby disclaims
any responsibility for them.*

iUniverse books may be ordered through booksellers or by contacting:

*iUniverse
1663 Liberty Drive
Bloomington, IN 47403
www.iuniverse.com
1-800-Authors (1-800-288-4677)*

*Because of the dynamic nature of the Internet, any Web addresses or links
contained in this book may have changed since publication and may no longer
be valid.*

*ISBN: 978-1-4401-3323-7 (pbk)
ISBN: 978-1-4401-3324-4 (ebk)*

Library of Congress Control Number: 2009925105

Printed in the United States of America

iUniverse rev. date: 4/6/2009

CONTENTS

INTRODUCTION

As a Chinese language professor, I have taught many classes at two prestigious American institutes, namely, the Monterey Institute of International Studies (MIIS), an affiliate of Middlebury College, as well as Defense Language Institute Foreign Language Center (DLIFLC). More often than not, I have found that American students and travelers take their own cultural baggage with them when they go to China, especially for the first time.

When I think about cultural differences, one thought-provoking anecdote (Axtell, 1993) always makes me smile, because it is so telling and emblematic of cultural differences:

> *Watching a Chinese person reverently placing fresh fruit on a grave, an American visitor asked, "When do you expect your ancestors to get up and eat the fruit?" The Chinese replied, "As soon as your ancestors get up and smell the flowers."*

I appreciate the humor found in such a situation, but also recognize that it is cultural differences that often separate us. Can we simply assume that all the values and traditions that people hold dear in America are equally important to Chinese? The answer, of course, is "No". We need to recognize that our own ways of doing things or dealing with others are actually conditioned in the cradle. We see our own ways as correct, and thus tend to judge people who do things differently, especially when they are from a different country. It is not uncommon to see a communication breakdown, misunderstanding or inappropriate behavior caused by a lack of knowledge of a particular culture. I firmly believe that raising cultural awareness is a necessity and should be an ongoing effort regardless of how much one already knows about a foreign language.

This book aims to provide Americans studying or traveling in China with a perspective and a reference. Although we may say that all Chinese people in China share certain values, beliefs, and characteristics, it is important to acknowledge that there can be significant differences in how these are exhibited in different regions, situations, or people, because there are many subcultures within the Chinese culture. My own particular background as a Beijing native undoubtedly affects my outlook. For example, this book presents the Chinese experience largely from the Beijing perspective, which is generally considered to be one of the mainstream cultures in China.

There are two parts to this book. Part I is a "cultural encounters" quiz which consists of two sections. In both sections multiple-choice questions illustrate common scenarios that foreign students or travelers are likely to experience when they are in China. Readers may use this part as a self-evaluation tool to measure their awareness of Chinese culture, especially with respect to studying or traveling there. Part II provides the answers and cultural briefings for the encounters that were listed in Part I.

Judy Zhu
Assistant Professor &
Diagnostic Assessment Specialist
Defense Language Institute Foreign
Language Center
Monterey, California, USA
February, 2009

Acknowledgements

Many people have contributed to this book. I am indebted to Mr. Leif Johnston, who reviewed and proofread the first and second draft and provided me with invaluable input and feedback.

I am also very grateful to Mr. Kevin Graham, Mr. John Berlin, Dr. Joel Young, Mr. Bruce McGlynn, and Mr. Steve Rawson for spending their valuable time reviewing and proofreading my third draft. My sincere thanks also go to Mr. Rick Crow, Ms. Sharon Danard, Mr. Leif Johnston, Mr. Wilfred Pi, Mr. Steve Collins, Miss Kate Collins, and Mr. John Morrison, who reviewed and proofread my final version before I submitted it to my publisher.

Last but not least, I own great debt to Dr. Ian Coats and Mr. Leif Johnston, who did the final proofing for my e-book version.

Judy Zhu

PART I: CULTURAL ENCOUNTERS QUIZ:

Instruction:

This quiz is divided into two sections. Section I focuses on student-teacher encounters. This section might be helpful for foreign students studying in China. Section II focuses on social encounters and it can be helpful for both foreign students and travelers. Please bear in mind that there could be more than one answer for each encounter, so select all that you think are appropriate.

Scoring scale/Comments:

Section I: (20 items in total)

Number of items that are answered correctly	Comments
20	You are truly an expert!
15-19	I am really impressed!
11-14	Very good.
6-10	Not bad, but I am sure you will do better after reading the book.
0-6	Let's read the book.

Section II: (80 items in total)

Number of items that were answered correctly	Comments
71-80	You are truly an expert!
61-70	Extremely impressive!
41-60	Excellent.
31-40	Very good.
21-30	Good.
11-20	Not bad.
0-10	Let's read the book now.

Section I: Student-Teacher Encounters

#1 When the teacher arrives in the classroom, it is best to:

A Remain seated and greet him/her.
B Stand up and bow.
C Stand up and shake hands
D Remain seated and wait until the teacher greets the class.

#2 When you are late for class, it is best to:

A Just come in and go to your seat.
B Knock first and then enter.
C Knock and wait for the teacher's permission to enter.
D Say "*Bao gao*" ("Report") first and then wait for the teacher to say "*Qing jin*" ("Come in").

#3 When your teacher doesn't show up, it is best to:

A Remain seated and wait quietly for at least 10 minutes.
B Go to the teacher's office to look for her/him.
C Go to other teachers' office to find a substitute.
D Go to the program head's office to report and ask what you need to do.

#4 When the teacher asks a question in class, it is best to:

A Answer it right away if you know the answer.
B Wait and see whom the teacher will call upon.
C Raise your hand if you know the answer.
D Make eye contact with the teacher if you know the answer.

#5 When you want to ask a question in class, it is best to:

A Ask your questions at any time.
B Wait until the teacher finishes talking.
C Raise your hand right away.
D Wait until the teacher asks if anyone has questions.

#6 When you want to eat or drink in class, it is best to:

A Ask the teacher before the class begins.
B Ask the teacher just before you do it.
C Just do it.
D Try to restrain yourself and wait until the next break.

#7 When the teacher gives you positive feedback in class, it is best to:

A Say "*Xiexie*" ("Thank you").
B Say "*Nali nali*" ("I am so flattered").
C Say nothing.
D Smile and nod.

#8 When the teacher pinpoints your mispronunciation or wrong grammar in front of others, it is best to:

A Say "*Xiexie*" ("Thank you").
B Say "*Dui bu qi*" ("I am sorry").
C Say nothing.
D Take note of what the teacher said.

#9 When there is too much homework, it is best to:

A Tell the teacher in front of the class.
B Tell the teacher in private after class.
C Tell the program head.
D Try your best to finish it.

#10 When class is over, it is best to:

A Say "*Xiexie*"("Thank you") to the teacher.
B Say "*Laoshi zaijian*" ("Goodbye, teacher").
C Tell the teacher how helpful the class was.
D Tell the teacher what you enjoyed the most.

#11 Giving gifts to teachers during the holidays,

A Is a common practice.
B Depends on whether or not you like the teacher.
C Is considered bribery.
D Should be approved by the program head first.

#12 Inviting your teacher to your apartment or out to a restaurant for dinner

A Is a common practice.
B Is considered bribery.
C Is acceptable.
D Should be approved by the program head in advance.

#13 When going to your teacher's office, it is best to:

A Simply go in.
B Knock on the door first and then go in.
C Knock on the door first and wait for permission to go in.
D Call the teacher's name and wait for permission to go in.

#14 When running into your teacher on campus while you are taking a walk, it is best to:

A Stop and chat a little bit after saying "Hi".
B Say "Hi", and then keep walking.
C Ignore him/her and keep walking.
D Stop and ask whether you could practice Chinese with him/her for a little while.

Judy Zhu

#15 When running into your teacher outside of school, it is best to:

A Chat a little bit after saying "*Laoshi hao*" (Hi teacher").
B Say "*Laoshi hao*" ("Hi teacher"), and then walk away.
C Nod your head to acknowledge him/her.
D Greet your teacher by shaking his/her hand.

#16 When being tutored by someone of the opposite sex outside the school, you could definitely:

A Date her/him.
B Invite her/him to dinner.
C Invite her/him to a movie.
D Pay extra once in a while to show your appreciation.

#17 When you do not like your teacher's teaching style, it is best to:

A Tell the teacher directly.
B Tell the program head.
C Ask an outspoken classmate to tell the teacher directly.
D Write a formal letter to the teacher and use indirect words to tell him/her.

#18 When you have a hard time understanding your teacher in class, it is best to:

A Ask the teacher to slow down right away.
B Bear with it and tell the teacher after class.
C Leave the classroom and take a short break.
D Ask the student next to you to explain to you.

#19 In China, Teachers' Day is on:

A August 8th.
B September 10th.
C November 11th.
D December 12th.

#20 When a teacher tells you that you should work harder, it is most likely that:

A The teacher thinks that you are lazy.
B The teacher is disappointed with your performance.
C The teacher does not like you and is trying to insult you.
D The teacher is doing her/his job to push you to the next level.

Section II: Social Encounters

Greetings

#1 When you are first introduced to Chinese people, you should:

A Shake hands with them.
B Hug them.
C Bow to them.
D Smile, stand there, and wait for them to initiate some action.

#2 When you walk on the street, it is best to:

A Say "*Ni hao*" ("Hi") to everyone who looks friendly.
B Say "*Ni hao*" ("Hi") back in Chinese when you are greeted with a "*Ni hao*" ("Hi").
C Extend your right hand to initiate a handshake to people who smile at you.
D Nod your head when people say "*Ni hao*" ("Hi") to you.

#3 When people ask you "*Chi le ma?*" ("Did you eat?") on the street, they often mean that:

A   They want to take you out to eat.
B   They want to invite you to a home-made dinner.
C   They are saying "Hi" to you.
D   They are curious.

Traffic and Directions

#4 When you try to cross a street, it is best to:

A Wait for the green light.
B Go with the flow even though there may be a red light.
C Start walking when you see a yellow light.
D Run no matter if it is a green light or red light.

#5 When you want to ask for directions on the street, the most efficient way is to:

A Say "*Laojia*" ("Excuse me") first to the person who is walking toward you.
B Go to the traffic policeman and ask for assistance.
C Always bring a map with you and show people where you want to go.
D Give a tip to the person that helped you.

Shopping

#6 When being surrounded by sales people for a product that you are not interested in, you should :

A Say "*Xiexie. Wo bu yao.*" ("Thank you. I do not want it") and then walk away.
B Ignore them and walk away.
C Take a look at the product and try it for the sake of being polite.
D Start bargaining to practice your bargaining skills even if you have no intention of buying.

#7 When returning a purchase at a store, you should:

A Go directly to the manager.
B Go to the cashier and show your invoice and purchase.
C Go to the counter where you purchased the item and do whatever the sales clerk says.
D Go to the counter where you purchased the item, if the sales clerk says "no", go to the manager.

#8 When your tour guide takes you to a store, you should always:

A Haggle and try to cut 60% off the price they offer.
B Believe what they say about the quality of the product or item.
C Buy a lot because they offer you a group discount.
D Ask your tour guide what you should buy.

#9 When you go to Silk Alley (Xiu Shui Market) in Beijing, you should always:

A Haggle.
B Go with a Chinese friend.
C Tell the vendors where you are from in order to get a discount.
D Make friends with the vendors first and then come back to shop.

#10 When you go to Red Bridge Market (Hong Qiao Market) in Beijing,

A   You should haggle.
B   You should go with a Chinese friend.
C   You can buy Chinese paintings, arts and crafts.
D   You might end up paying 1/3 of the price that the vendors ask for.

#11 When a person tries to sell you DVDs/CDs on the street, it is best to:

A Say "*Xiexie. Wo bu yao.*" ("Thanks. I do not want them.") and walk away.
B Stop and take a look at the selection.
C Haggle for a lower price.
D Ask the person whether or not the DVDs/CDs are pirated.

#12 When a person on the street offers to take you to her/his store to select DVDs/CDs, it is best to:

A Say "*Xiexie. Wo bu yao.*" ("Thanks. I do not want them.") and walk away.
B Go with the person and take a look at the selection.
C Haggle before you go with him/her.
D Ask the person whether or not the DVDs/CDs are pirated before you go with him/her.

Dining out and social gatherings

#13 When going to a birthday party, it is best to:

A Ask the birthday girl/boy what she/he wants, so that you could get the person a gift she/he desires.
B Bring a gift worth 100 *Yuan* (about $14.70) or above.
C Bring any gift that shows a token of care and love from you.
D Bring a bottle of wine or a birthday cake.

#14 When having dinner with a local family, it is best to:

A Ask the host what you should bring.
B Bring fruit or health products.
C Bring a prepared dish or other food.
D Bring a bottle of wine.

#15 When being offered some food that you do not like to eat, it is best to:

A Try one bite and say you do not like it.
B Tell the person that you do not like it so that no one will offer it again.
C Tell the person that you are allergic to it.
D Just eat it to show your politeness.

#16 When friends keep asking you to drink alcohol and you do not want to drink, it is best to:

A Try a little and say that it is too strong for you.
B Keep drinking to please them.
C Explain that you do not drink and then offer to use water or soda instead.
D Explain that you do not drink and then just watch them drink.

#17 When you dine out with Chinese friends, the most common practice is:

A You pay because you are an American and Americans are always considered rich.
B Your friends pay to show their hospitality because you are a foreign visitor.
C You go Dutch with your friends.
D The person who initiated the dinner/get-together pays because he/she is the organizer.

#18 When a friend tries to pay for a meal, you could:

A Let your friend pay and thank him/her.
B Tell him/her that he/she does not have to, and you do not mind going Dutch.
C Tell him/her that he/she does not have to, and you do not mind buying.
D Say "no" and insist that you pay.

#19 The main staple on a dinner table in China can be:

A Rice
B Noodles
C Bread
D Potatoes

#20 Should you wait to be seated at a restaurant?

A Always.
B Not at all.
C It depends on the restaurant.
D It depends on how many people will eat.

#21 When you order food at a restaurant, you are often expected to:

A Order an appetizer first, and then soup and an entrée.
B Order soup first, and then an appetizer and entrée.
C Ask the server to make some recommendations.
D Order whatever you want regardless of the order you intend to eat it in.

#22 After you place an order at a restaurant, it is best to:

A Expect anything to come first (entrée, soup, appetizers, etc).
B Expect appetizers to come first.
C Expect soup to come first.
D Expect to wait for 30 minutes or even longer to get the food.

#23 When you need more drinks or more tea at a restaurant, you could:

A Expect the server to refill your soft drink automatically.
B Ask the server to refill your soft drink for free.
C Order another soft drink.
D Put the lid of the tea pot upside down and leave a little opening.

#24 When people smoke at the restaurant and it bothers you, you could:

A Ask them to stop smoking.
B Ask a server to move you to a non-smoking area.
C Ask a server to ask them to stop smoking.
D Complain to the restaurant manager.

#25 When you hear people talking loudly at a restaurant, it is best to:

A Go to them and ask them to lower their voice.
B Ask a server to tell them to lower their voice.
C Put up with them.
D Complain to the restaurant manager.

#26 When you finish eating and are ready to pay the bill,

A You should ask the server to bring the check.
B Go to the host/cashier to get the check yourself.
C Always double check the bill before you pay.
D Ask the server whether a tip is needed or not.

#27 When you pay for the meal at a restaurant,

A You can use a personal check.
B You should include a 15%-20% tip.
C You can always use a credit card.
D You can always ask for a receipt/invoice.

#28 What utensils do most Chinese people use when they eat?

A Fork and knife
B Spoon
C Chopsticks
D Hands

#29 When you are served with a hot or cold cloth towel, it is meant to:

A Wash your face.
B Wash your hands.
C Wipe the table after dinner.
D Use it to hold a hot plate or glass.

#30 After dinner, most of Chinese:

A Floss.
B Use toothpicks.
C Go to the bathroom to brush their teeth.
D Go to the bathroom to rinse their mouth.

#31 When a Chinese person uses the chopsticks he/she eats with to serve you,

A It is not considered rude.
B It is considered rude.
C You could ask the person to use a pair of serving chopsticks.
D You could ask the person to use a serving spoon.

#32 Which of the following is the most common and acceptable table manner in China?

A Belching.
B Talking loudly with food in one's mouth.
C Keeping one's mouth closed and not talking when eating.
D Blowing one's nose

#33 When you go to a night market for dinner, it is better to:

A Be prepared to see BBQ scorpion.
B Be prepared to bargain.
C Drink some liquor after eating any food.
D Try not to eat anything there.

#34 When you go to a bar,

A You need to show your passport.
B You might have to pay 40 *Yuan* (about $6) or more for a bottle of beer.
C You should give a tip.
D You can hit on whomever you want.

#35 When accepting a formal invitation, it is best to:

A Send a written message by mail.
B Call and tell the host verbally.
C Send a written message by email.
D Tell the inviter in person.

#36 When you go to a wedding, the best thing that you can do to make the newly-weds happy is to:

A Dress formally and bring a nice gift.
B Give a "red envelope" with cash inside as a wedding gift.
C Come with your spouse or date.
D Help clean up afterwards.

#37 If you can not make it to your friend's wedding ceremony and reception,

A You should still buy a nice wedding gift.
B You should take the newly-wed to dinner within a month of their wedding ceremony.
C You should go to their apartment or house to visit them.
D You do not have to do anything.

Transportation and travel

#38 If the car behind you honks when you drive, or ride a taxi, you should:

A Ignore it.
B Check through the rear mirror and see what happened.
C Stop and ask the driver what's the matter.
D Wave and continue driving or riding.

#39 With an American driver's license, you could:

A Drive a friend's car if the car is insured.
B Rent a car.
C Rent a bike.
D Rent a motorcycle.

#40 While riding a public bus, you are expected to:

A Give your seat to an elderly person.
B Give your seat to a pregnant woman.
C Give your seat to a woman who is holding a baby.
D Follow the "first come, first serve" rule when it comes to seating.

#41 When you take a taxi, you should:

A Tip the driver when you pay.
B Ask the driver to use the meter right after you get in.
C Ask the driver to give you an official invoice/receipt after you pay.
D Not expect the driver to give you any change.

#42 If a man offers you taxi service, but you do not see a "taxi" sign on his car, it is best to:

A Thank him and then walk away.
B Haggle and get a good price before you hop in.
C Ignore him.
D Ask a Chinese friend whether or not you should take it.

#43 The normal practice of getting a taxi is to:

A Call a taxi company first and wait to be picked up at a place you prefer.
B Go to a taxi stop to wait for one.
C Wave to any taxi on the street.
D Wave to any taxi that has a sign of "vacant".

#44 If you are at a scenic spot and you are asked by a Chinese person to take a picture with you, it is most likely that:

A You are considered a terrorist and the Chinese government is monitoring you.
B The person is trying to be friends with you.
C The person thinks it is cool to have a picture with Westerners.
D The person is trying to use this as a means to network with you.

#45 When you want to take a picture or record some videos in a supermarket:

A You should always ask the clerk first.
B You can do so if you do not see any sign that prohibits it.
C You should ask your Chinese friend or tour guide first.
D You can do so if you can make sure to not have any people in your picture or video.

#46 When it comes time to use a public bathroom, it is wise to:

A Bring tissues with you.
B Be prepared that public bathrooms are generally filthy.
C Be prepared that you might not have the regular toilet that you are used to.
D Be prepared to pay.

#47 If you travel in the countryside and the locals stare at you without saying anything, that means:

A You are considered an intruder and they do not welcome you.
B They are scared of you.
C They do not know how to interact with you.
D They are curious about who you are and where you are from.

Names

#48 What do you know about Chinese names?

A Family names go first, then the given name.
B Women will change their surname to their husbands' when they get married.
C Children always inherit their father's surname.
D Some Chinese pay specialists to give their child a meaningful name.

#49 When you address the father/mother of your friend, you could use:

A Uncle/Aunt.
B Mr/Mrs.
C Their first names.
D Their full names.

Customs and social practices

#50 When your Chinese friend gives you a present, the most common practice in China is to:

A Open it right away.
B Ask the friend whether you could open it right away.
C Say "*Wo bu neng yao*" ("I can not accept it") several times before you accept it.
D Not open it in front of your friend.

#51 When you consider buying a gift for a friend, what would not be acceptable?

A A carton of brand name cigarettes if your friend smokes.
B Brand name liquor or wine if your friend drinks.
C A fancy clock for an elderly friend.
D Toys for their child.

#52 When you give a gift to a Chinese friend, you should:

A Wrap it nicely.
B Expect the friend to open it right away.
C Emphasize that the gift is small, but it is a token of appreciation/love/care.
D Take off the price tag.

#53 Which of the following items should not be given to Chinese people as a gift?

A Chopticks.
B Knives.
C Green hats.
D Red shirts.

#54 When asking for a favor, you should:

A Use the word "*qing*" ("please").
B Use the phrase "*Keyi mafan ni...?*" ("May I trouble you to …?")
C Promise to give something in return afterwards.
D Promise to give something in return before hand.

#55 When a Chinese friend goes the extra mile to drive you around, you could:

A Offer to pay the gas money.
B Treat your friend to a nice dinner at McDonalds or KFC.
C Buy a nice gift for your friend.
D Thank your friend verbally.

#56 Karaoke:

A Is often used for prostitution.
B Is often used for "after hours" businesses networking or negotiations.
C Is often used during family get-togethers.
D Is a popular way to welcome foreign guests.

#57   When Chinese people ask you to deliver a song at a Karaoke club, they are most likely to:

A   Ask you to sing an English song.
B   Ask you to sing a Chinese song.
C   Push you to sing several times.
D   Stop asking if you say that you are off-key.

#58 When you have a dinner appointment with a friend at 6: 30 p.m. and it's already 7: 00 p.m. and you haven't seen or heard from your friend yet, you could:

A Go ahead and eat by yourself.
B Leave because he/she is rude.
C Call the friend's spouse or other friends.
D Call the friend.

#59 When receiving and presenting a name card, you should:

A Use both hands.
B Use your right hand.
C Use your left hand.
D Use whatever hand you are comfortable with because it does not matter.

#60 After you receive a name card, the most appropriate thing to do is to:

A Shove it into your pocket.
B Put it on the table so that you can refer to it later.
C Put it in your name card holder.
D Return it to the person after you have read it.

#61 When a Chinese friend asks about your salary or how much your house in the States costs, it means:

A The friend is thinking of how much money he/she should spend on buying you a gift.
B The friend is running out of topics to discuss.
C The friend is curious.
D The friend is considering who should pay the bill when you dine out together.

#62 When being complimented, it is best to:

A Be happy and show your appreciation by saying "*Xiexie*" ("Thank you").
B Be humble and show your modesty by saying "You are too kind" or "I am flattered".
C Smile and say nothing.
D Compliment them back.

#63 When an elderly gets on a bus and you want to give him/her your seat, it is best to:

A Smile at the senior and wait until he/she walks toward your direction.
B Tell the ticket conductor before or while you stand up.
C Wave at the elderly and motion for him/her to come to you.
D Just stand up and make the seat available.

#64 If you are a man and are going to a movie with a Chinese girl, you are expected to:

A Buy the tickets for the two of you and drinks and snacks as well.
B Buy the ticket and drinks just for yourself.
C Wait and see what the girl wants you to do.
D Offer to buy the tickets and ask the girl to buy drinks and snacks.

#65 When going to a movie, you are expected to:

A Follow the "first come, first serve" principle and sit wherever you want.
B Sit where your ticket says.
C Ask your neighbor to switch seats with you.
D Introduce yourself to the people who are next to you.

#66 When watching a movie with your Chinese date at a movie theatre, you often are not expected to:

A Hold her/his hands.
B Kiss her/him.
C Hold her/him tight.
D Ignore her/him and just focus on the movie.

#67 When a Chinese person sneezes, others will normally say:

A "*Shangdi baoyou ni*" ("God bless you.").
B "*You ren xiang ni*" ("Someone is missing you.").
C "*Yibai sui*" ("Live up to 100 years old.").
D Nothing.

#68 A 40 year old man that lives in his parents' house without paying rent is considered:

A A loser in society.
B Ok.
C Selfish.
D Cheap.

Hand gestures and body language

#69 What does it mean when a Chinese person gives you the middle finger?

A An insult.
B Respect.
C The number one.
D Nothing.

Street phenomenon

#70 Two young men holding each other' shoulders in public are most likely:

A Colleagues.
B Homosexual.
C Brothers.
D Good friends.

#71 Two women holding hands in public are most likely:

A Lesbians.
B Relatives.
C Sisters.
D Good friends.

#72 A Man and a woman, who are about the same age and hold hands in pubic, are most likely:

A A couple.
B Good friends.
C Brother and sister.
D Friends with benefits.

#73 When a same sex Chinese person puts an arm across your shoulders or pats you on your back, it means:

A Sexual harassment.
B Intent to date you.
C Intent to show friendliness.
D Lack of respect.

#74 When you see people fight in the front of a store, it is best to:

A Mind your own business.
B Ask the reasons and try to mediate.
C Find the security guard of the store and let him/her handle it.
D Call 911.

#75 If you see a man spank his child in public and you think it is abuse, you should:

A Call 911.
B Mind your own business.
C Call 110.
D Ask him why and tell him to have non-violent communication with his child.

#76 If you see a child/beggar coming to you asking for money on the street, it is best to:

A Give some money to the child.
B Ignore the child.
C Give some food to the child.
D Talk with the child and ask him about his family.

#77 When people smoke on the street, which of the followings will happen?

A They will be fined.
B They will get a verbal warning from the traffic policeman on duty.
C Some people will call 120.
D Nothing.

#78 When you see people spit on street, you should:

A Tell the person not to do so.
B Ignore the person.
C Tell a patrol officer or a traffic police.
D Call 120.

Safety and medical treatment

#79 If you go to a crowded place during the day time, you should:

A Only carry travelers checks with you.
B Have a backpack or briefcase with your wallet inside.
C Take a limited amount of cash and carry it with you.
D Only take your credit card and ID with you.

#80 If you are sick and do not know what's wrong, you should:

A Go to the US Embassy or a US consulate.
B Call a Chinese friend or your tour guide to take you to the hospital.
C Take medication that your tour guide gives to you.
D Take medication that your friend gives to you.

Part II Answers to Chinese Cultural Encounters Quiz and Cultural Aspects Briefings

Answer key for Section I: Student – Teacher Encounters:

Item Number	Answers
#1	D
#2	C
#3	A
#4	C
#5	D
#6	D
#7	C
#8	D
#9	D
#10	A
#11	A
#12	C
#13	C
#14	B
#15	A
#16	B
#17	B
#18	B
#19	B
#20	D

Answer Key for Section II: Social Encounters

Item Number	Answers
#1	A
#2	B
#3	C
#4	B
#5	B
#6	A
#7	C
#8	A
#9	A
#10	A, C, D
#11	A
#12	A
#13	B
#14	B
#15	C
#16	C
#17	D
#18	D
#19	A, B
#20	C
#21	D
#22	A
#23	C, D
#24	B
#25	C
#26	A, C
#27	D

#28	C
#29	B
#30	B
#31	A
#32	B
#33	A, B, C
#34	B
#35	B
#36	B
#37	A
#38	B
#39	C
#40	A, B, C
#41	C
#42	A
#43	D
#44	C
#45	A
#46	A, B, C, D
#47	C, D
#48	A, D
#49	A, B
#50	D
#51	C
#52	A, C
#53	C
#54	B
#55	B, C, D
#56	B, C
#57	C

#58	D
#59	A
#60	C
#61	C
#62	B
#63	B
#64	A
#65	B
#66	D
#67	B
#68	B
#69	D
#70	D
#71	D
#72	A
#73	C
#74	C
#75	B
#76	C
#77	D
#78	B
#79	C
#80	B

CULTURAL ASPECTS AND BRIEFINGS

What is Culture?

Chaney and Martin (2000) define culture as the structure through which communication is formulated and interpreted in society. Indeed, culture deals with the many ways people live, behave and think.

People who were born and raised in different countries can seemingly have different values and codes of conduct due to cultural differences. No two individuals view the external world the same way (Singer, 1998). For example, Chinese people greatly value their group and their family. Therefore, it is important for them to follow family traditions and the wishes of their parents and even grandparents, while Americans might consider it a sign of lack of assertiveness. In a similar way, the value that Americans place on individualism, is often perceived as self-centered by Chinese. Therefore, the importance of acknowledging the differences between cultures cannot be overemphasized. Each culture has its own unique values and virtues. There is no good or bad culture in the world; there are only differences. Being able to embrace other cultures instead of judging them is the first step for a fruitful journey of foreign language learning or a pleasant trip to a foreign land.

Basic Facts about China

With an area of 9.6 million square kilometers (about 3.7 million square miles), China is the fourth largest country in the world. Beijing, known as Peking in the past, is the capital.

With Han as a majority counting for 94% of the total population of 1.3 billion, there are 56 different ethnic groups in China. Although most Chinese from the mainland are taught to be atheist, some religions, such as Taoism, Buddhism, Christianity, and Islam, are also commonly practiced. Among these religions, Buddhism, with an estimated 100 million adherents, is the most widely practiced, according to CIA *World Fact Book* statistics.

Mandarin Chinese, which is also known as Putonghua, is the official language of China. Shanghai, Guangzhou and Hong Kong are well known for their own dialects. Specifically, Shanghai natives speak Shanghainese among themselves, while people who are from Guangzhou and Hong Kong speak Cantonese. Meanwhile, some English words have been widely adopted by Chinese, such as "ok" and "bye-bye." The writing script uses *hanzi,* which are the Chinese characters. Throughout Chinese history, more than 80,000 characters have been identified and about 11,000 of them are still in use today. However, only about 3,500 characters are commonly used in day to day communication.

Chinese currency is called *Renminbi* (RMB) – literally "the people's currency." The basic unit of RMB is the *yuan*, which is the Chinese dollar. While referred to as *yuan* in the written form, in spoken language, the word *kuai* is used. Each *yuan* or *kuai* is composed of 10 *jiao* or *mao*, which is a Chinese dime. The smallest denomination is the *fen*, 100 of which make a *yuan.*

Student-Teacher Encounter Briefings

Dos and Don'ts:

DO raise your right hand to answer or ask a question.

DO knock and wait for the teacher's permission to come in when you are late for class.

DO knock when you go to a teacher's office.

DO thank the teacher after a class.

DO feel free to give your teacher a gift during the holidays.

DO greet your teachers when you run into them outside of class.

DO NOT eat or drink in the classroom.

DO NOT say "Thank you" when a teacher gives you positive feedback.

DO NOT react and tell a teacher on the spot if you don't agree with the teacher's comments.

DO NOT date your tutor unless it is not against any rules.

DO NOT tell your teacher that her or his teaching style does not work for you.

DO NOT interrupt your teachers.

DO NOT tell a teacher to slow down in front of the class.

#1 When the teacher arrives in the classroom:

The traditions and customs for this have changed over the past 20 years. In the past, when a teacher walked into a classroom, the class leader would say "*qi li*" ("stand up") and the entire class would stand up and greet the teacher by saying *"Laoshi hao."* With China's opening up and reform that was implemented in late 1970s, more and more Chinese schools have been exposed to Western educational systems. Today, although most of the public Chinese schools, such as elementary and high schools, still practice this tradition, some have become more flexible, especially when there is a full room of foreign students. For example, students could remain seated and wait until the teacher says something before responding. On the other hand, specific rules vary from school to school. Therefore, it is important to check with the school that you are going to study at and do what they recommend.

#2 When you are late for a class:

Rules which apply to this have changed over the past 20 years. Some schools still demand that students say *"baogao"* ("Report") first and then wait for the teacher to let them in. In this case, a teacher may demand an explanation for why you are late.

On the other hand, if you are in a Chinese language class with a group of other non-Chinese students, you are often exempt from these rules with the notion that Chinese customs should not be imposed on foreign students. Therefore, knocking and waiting for the teacher's permission to enter is a common and polite way to handle this situation. You may also come in quietly and go directly to your seat. However, you are expected to go to the teacher right away to provide her or him with an explanation as to why you are late.

#3 When your teacher is late for a class:

In China, if a teacher doesn't show up when the class starts, most of the time students will wait patiently for the teacher to arrive and some may start to self-study. If a teacher hasn't shown up after 10 minutes, the class leader or a volunteer may go to the teacher's office to look for her or him. If the teacher is not found or can not be reached by phone, one can go to the program head's office to report and the program head will find a substitute teacher. Students are not expected to ask any other teacher for substitution. It is not acceptable for a student to leave because the teacher is 15 minutes late.

#4 When the teacher asks a question in class:

It is always polite to raise your right hand if you want to answer a question. Sometimes, a teacher might ask someone to answer a question when they have made direct eye contact. A teacher might also call on someone to answer a question at his or her own will. It is considered rude to answer a teacher's question without first being called upon. In Chinese culture, a teacher is considered the authority of a classroom as well as the authority of a subject that he or she teaches. Interrupting a teacher or answering a question without being called indicates a lack of respect for authority.

#5 When you want to ask a question in class:

In the Chinese culture, it is very important to show your respect to teachers. Confucius (551-479 BC), China's famous teacher, philosopher, and political theorist, once asked, "Without feelings of respect, what is there to distinguish men from beasts?" Chinese are raised with the notion that teachers are the ones who empower and enlighten people, and people should always admire, respect and appreciate teachers' knowledge and work. A Chinese saying goes as "*Yi ri wei shi, zhong sheng wei fu.*" ("Even if a man only serves as your teacher for a day, he should be considered as important as your father who gives you life.") One rule of thumb is to never interrupt a teacher while he or she is talking or giving a lecture. This means holding questions until the teacher has finished speaking and has asked if anyone has a question. You might then raise your right hand and wait to be called upon before asking your question.

#6 When you want to eat or drink in class:

All students are expected to be attentive in the classroom. Disruptive behavior, such as eating or drinking, are not allowed. If you really need to eat or drink, you will have to talk with your teacher before the class begins. Otherwise, you can be seen as a rude and ill-mannered American. It will not only affect your teacher's impression of you personally, but also possibly that of your compatriots.

#7 & #8 When your teacher gives you positive or negative feedback in class:

Chinese students are not expected to respond to a teacher's feedback. Teacher-student communication is often one way – the teacher gives feedback and students listen. The feedback, whether positive or negative, could be given in front of a whole class or in private.

If the feedback is positive, you can simply nod and say nothing. Smiling is nice, but you are not expected to do so since most of the feedback is given in a formal or serious fashion. What you are expected to do is to be attentive.

Saying "*Xiexie*" ("Thank you") back to your Chinese teacher will be considered arrogant or complacent, which is not desired in Chinese culture. On the other hand, if a teacher points out your academic weaknesses in front of others, do not be offended. This is a normal practice in China. Teachers are seen as the authority in terms of the subject matter they teach. Criticizing you does not equate to putting you down or insulting you. Rather, it is a long term teaching tradition in China that is based on the concept that "excellent students can only be produced by tough teachers." The best approach is to nod and take note of what the teacher says. If you do not agree with the teacher's comments, do not react and tell the teacher on the spot – it will be considered disrespectful. Instead, talk to the teacher or program head after class, though most Chinese students will simply accept the feedback or share their feelings with their friends. Talking to the teacher after class as an American student does is not practiced in China. Both Chinese students and teachers see this behavior as challenging an authority and a lack of humbleness.

#9 When there is too much homework:

In China teachers do not reduce the amount of homework because of students' complaints or concerns. It is always considered necessary to do tons of homework after class in order to succeed in a program. Therefore, don't be surprised by a heavy workload. Try to be positive and realize that when you have more homework, the teacher actually will have more to grade and critique as well. If you negotiate the amount of homework with the teacher, you might be considered a lazy American who does not have respect for that teacher unless the teacher is very familiar with American culture and its educational system.

#10 When class is over:

It is always considered polite and well-mannered when you thank a teacher after a class. Saying goodbye to your teacher after class is also a good way to show your respect to the teacher, but it is not expected by every teacher. Telling a teacher how helpful the class is or what you enjoyed the most is not a common practice in China. Some teachers might welcome it, while others might think you are condescending by putting yourself in a position to judge a professional instructor.

#11 *Giving gifts to teachers during the holidays:*

It is a common practice to give teachers gifts during the holidays. The New Year, Spring Festival (Chinese lunar New Year) and Teacher's Day are the holidays that teachers most often receive gifts from students. Most students like to give teachers wall calendars on the New Year. Some other popular gifts include flowers, cards, health care products, books, and so forth. Students are not supposed to give a teacher an expensive item as a gift – that may make teachers feel like they are being bribed. For example, if a student gives a teacher a brand name watch that costs $680 *yuan* (about $100), the teacher could feel very uncomfortable.

#12 *Inviting your teacher to your apartment or restaurant for dinner:*

This is not a common practice. However, it is quite acceptable. During the winter or summer break after your grade has been given, it is completely fine to invite a teacher to your apartment or restaurant for dinner, especially when you ask for a letter of recommendation for further education. It is not common for one student to invite all of his or her teachers for dinner though. No one in the Chinese culture will consider taking a teacher out for dinner to be a "bribe" or to indicate some ulterior motive unless you are asking for a better grade. Chinese like to show their appreciation to teachers, friends or family members by treating them to a good meal at a restaurant.

#13 *When going to your teacher's office:*

Knocking at the door and waiting for the teacher's permission to enter is a common practice. Sometimes, if a teacher shares a big office with a few other teachers and the door is open, it will be acceptable for you to call the teacher's name at the door to get his or her attention before going in.

However, this is not the preferred approach by most teachers, because they feel that they are being notified instead of being asked for permission, which is a sign of respect. Therefore, it is best to always knock at the door first.

#14 & #15 When running into your teacher outside of the classroom:

You are expected to say "*Laoshi hao*" ("hi teacher") to your teachers any time that you run into them. This is a sign of good manners and respect in the Chinese culture. Ignoring or avoiding teachers is seen as a sign of disrespect. Nowadays younger Chinese tend to introduce any friends or family members that they are with to their teacher; however, older Chinese often do not do so, because this was not practiced when they were raised.

When you see a teacher on campus, it is common to keep walking after a brief "*Laoshi hao*." ("hi teacher"). Teachers normally only have ten minutes break between classes, and even if they do not teach in the next ten minutes, they will be busy with administrative work or lesson preparations. Stopping to chat is not recommended. You are expected to go to the teacher's office if you have a concern or question. Of course, this is the general rule and is what is preferred by most teachers in China. It can vary from teacher to teacher as well. In short, if you do stop to chat with a teacher, he or she will probably do so in order to be polite.

If you bump into your teacher off-campus, such as at a store, a restaurant, or a bank, a common practice is to say "hi" in Chinese and to chat for a little bit if time permits. It is considered rude if you do not greet your teacher when you see him or her unless the circumstance does not allow you to do so.

#16 When having a tutor of the opposite sex:

It is not uncommon to have a tutor if you are learning Chinese in China. The tutor could be recommended by your school or by your friends. The tutor could also be a professional teacher that is paid on an hourly basis, or even a student who simply wants to do a language exchange.

You should not date your tutor if the tutor is assigned or recommended by your school and is a professional teacher or a student at your school, because this might affect the professional relationship between you and your tutor or the program. Most of the Chinese language programs try to make this rule clear at the beginning of their course. However, reality is not always as perfect as we might wish. You might hear a rumor or know that in your program a foreign student dated a school-assigned tutor and there were no disciplinary consequences. This does not make it right for you to do so, though. On the other hand, inviting a tutor to dinner is considered a way to build up friendship or to show appreciation. Therefore, it is accepted and will not be considered dating unless you show sexual interest, though inviting a tutor of the opposite sex to a movie is generally considered a date by Chinese.

If the tutor is recommended by your friend and is not from your school, you may date him or her as you wish. Nevertheless, despite your wish to make progress in your language proficiency, going out with your tutor might result in a lack of focus – you might end up speaking English a lot in order to communicate more effectively. It is not necessarily bad, but you may need to be prepared for the consequences.

Paying extra once in a while is not necessary and can be counter-productive, because the tutor might either have more expectations in the future or feel uncomfortable.

#17 When you do not like your teacher's teaching style:

Chinese people put a high value on dignity. *"Diu lian"* or *"Mei mianzi"* are typical Chinese phrases describing losing one's dignity. These two phrases translate into "losing face" in English. From elementary school onward, Chinese people are instilled with the notion that "losing face" means losing dignity and that once dignity is lost, one can hardly get it back, sometimes never.

Every teacher has his or her unique personality and teaching style. Sometimes it just boils down to whether or not your teacher's style suits yours. Teachers have always been highly respected in the Chinese culture. If you go to a teacher and tell him or her that their teaching style does not work for you, regardless of your intentions, the teacher may feel like he or she "has lost face". This may result in an uncomfortable situation or their being resentful.

Telling the program head is the best option you could use if you cannot adjust your learning strategy to better suit the teaching style. However, you have to be careful with your words and tone. Bear in mind that you do not want your communication to be mistaken as a complaint. Later on, the teacher may hold a grudge and the program head would consider you a troublemaker.

If your teacher has expressed his or her willingness to accept feedback from students (which is unusual in Chinese culture), writing a formal letter to the teacher using appreciative words to show your respect and gratitude can be a good way to get your point across. In the letter you may explain your learning style and indirectly let the teacher know what he or she could do to further contribute to your learning. The teacher will have dignity in front of others and might reflect without feeling that he or she "has lost face". Therefore, there

Judy Zhu

is a better chance for you to maintain a good relationship with the teacher.

#18 When you have a hard time understanding your teacher in class:

It might be acceptable if you ask the teacher to slow down right away, depending on the teacher's personality type and preferences. Bear in mind that this is for your immediate benefit. Most teachers will react professionally. However, there is no guarantee that the teacher will not feel that he or she is "losing face" or being disrespected. Given each individual's unique personality, I would encourage you to react to this situation accordingly. Sometimes it is polite and beneficial to bear with the teacher's accent and to try to take notes from the blackboard or from your classmates.

If you feel the need to let the teacher know, the best approach is to tell the teacher in private after class, yet in a very polite and indirect way. For example, you might ask the teacher what he or she thinks about the reasons why you have a hard time understanding his or her lecture. You might also ask for a handout or written outline of the course content and tell him or her why you are doing so.

#19 China's Teacher's Day:

Teacher's Day in China is currently celebrated on September 10th. However, in the modern Chinese history, it has been celebrated on three different dates.

In 1932, during the period of the Republic of China, June 6th was set as Teacher's Day to show appreciation and respect for teachers. After the People's Republic of China was founded on Oct 1st 1949, Teacher's Day was moved to May 1st, which is also the International Labor Day. Finally, on January 21st, 1985, the Standing Committee of China's National

People's Congress passed a bill proclaiming September 10th to be Teacher's Day, and it has been observed nationwide since then. On this day, students often show their respect and appreciation in various ways, such as buying a card or flowers. Most schools, especially public schools, give teachers half the day off.

#20 When a teacher tells you that you should work harder:

Similar to Americans, Chinese also believe that hard work is the basis for success. As the Chinese idiom goes, "*Ben niao xian fei*" ("A slow bird will be ahead if it starts early and persistently tries hard"). Chinese parents and teachers strongly believe that pushing students to work hard is very important regardless of where the students stand academically. Therefore, it is very common to overhear a teacher tell a student to work harder, even though that student is already in the top five. When teachers stop pushing a student, they are considered to not be doing their jobs.

Additional comments:

Within the Chinese culture, there are many subcultures within a region or a school. It will be helpful to keep an open mind when going to China to learn the language and culture. Student-teacher encounters can vary from region to region, school to school, or even person to person. Therefore, learning and adapting to the culture and people you encounter instead of judging or rejecting them based on your own culture is the ultimate goal that I would recommend.

Social Encounter Briefings:

Greetings – refer to questions #1 to #3

<u>Dos and Don'ts:</u>

DO give a firm and long handshake when you are introduced to a Chinese person for the first time.

DO NOT shake hands with a glove on or with one hand in a pocket.

DO NOT bow.

Although Chinese might bow when they want to show their deep gratitude to someone, they do not bow when they greet one another. Rather, shaking hands is a common practice, especially when they are first introduced to each other. The firmness and length of handshakes can vary due to factors like gender, social status, age, and personality types. Generally speaking, a firm and longer handshake with a genuine slight smile shows sincerity to Chinese. Never shake hands with a glove on or with one hand in a pocket, because this is considered disrespectful.

When Westerners initiate a hug, most Chinese will accept it, but they do not initiate it. On the other hand, those who are educated and have lived in the Western cultures for a certain period of time might feel more comfortable to hug or even initiate one.

While "*Ni hao*" ("hi") or "*Ni hao ma?*" ("How are you?") are the most common greetings that Westerners have heard or learned, there are a lot variations in the real world. I once carried out a study on variations in how Chinese people greet each other. The results of my data actually shocked me as a native speaker of Chinese and a professional Chinese language instructor. There are just too many ways to greet each other depending on different social variables, such as gender, age, occupation, social class and origin. Generally speaking, greetings between colleagues appear to have some kind of socializing element, such as catching up with one another by asking "*Zhoumo zenmeyang?*" ("How was your weekend?) or "*Zuijin mang ba?*" ("You have been pretty busy lately, I suppose?"), while greetings between acquaintances or friends tend to be more casual and they are more or less similar to a simple "hi" in English. Such a pattern can probably be attributed to the courtesy levels among coworkers and friends. Therefore, it is safe and polite to say "*Ni hao*" ("hi") whether shaking hands with the person whom you are introduced to or when greeted by a friendly Chinese on the street. On the other hand, if the person is much older than you or has a much higher social status, then "*Nin hao*"("hi") instead of "*Ni hao*" ("hi") should be used, because the former shows more respect.

However, Chinese generally do not greet strangers on the street, because this is not taught at school or home. Also, there are simply too many people on the street. Additionally, because of some con games and sales promotions on the street, many Chinese tend to think that the person saying hello has some ulterior motive. Therefore, even though you may see some Chinese that look friendly and have direct eye contact with you, it is best not to say "*Ni hao*" to them unless you know them or have met them before. If you do greet them, chances are you will get a puzzled look accompanied with silence, or at best, a smile. In certain areas, such as in the country, some Chinese might greet you by saying "*Ni hao*" or "*Hello*"even though they do not know you. They may also ask their child to say "*Hello*" to you. This is because they want to be friendly to foreign visitors or they are just curious about you. In this situation, you definitely should say "*Ni hao*" back.

If you ask someone in the US whether they've eaten yet it's because you might want them to join you for lunch or dinner. In China, however, "*Chi le ma?*" ("Did you eat?") is a very common greeting among friends, colleagues, and acquaintances when they frequently run into each other. Often they greet one another with this and keep walking. The response does not matter to the greeter, because this is more of an informal and personal "*Ni hao*" instead of asking whether the greeted have eaten or not. Despite the nature of this greeting, one will not say "*Ni hao*" back. Rather, "*Ai*" ("Yup"), "*Chi le*" ("Yeah, I did") or "*Mei ne*" ("Not yet") are three typical responses.

Traffic and directions – refer to questions #4 & #5

Dos and Don'ts:

DO always bring a map of the local area with you.

DO NOT always wait for a green light.

China is a country with a population of 1.3 billion. The reinforcement of traffic rules and regulations in cities such as Beijing, which has 12 million people, has seen some progress, but the reality is still harsh – in some districts you will see people cross the street even though there is a red light. You will also see drivers make right turns when they are not supposed to. It is true that you should abide by the traffic laws and rules, but under those circumstances, waiting for a green light or crossing the street while a car is supposed to yield will only put you in danger. Therefore, going with the flow is always the best approach in China. Otherwise, you will never get a chance to cross the street given the huge number of cars, bicycles, and pedestrians as well as how the traffic laws are followed and enforced in a particular area.

When asking for directions it is always helpful to first say "excuse me" in Chinese (useful common Chinese phrases can be found in Appendix I). However, if you forget how to say the word, you might simply show someone your map and point at the place that you want to go. Chinese people generally like to help; you will get detailed directions if the person whom you ask knows. On the other hand, since there are a lot of people from out-of-town in such big cities as Beijing and Shanghai, it will be more efficient to ask the traffic policeman for directions. They either stand on a round center stage in the middle of an intersection, or they sit in an enclosed traffic pavilion at a corner of an intersection. They do not necessarily speak English well, but they direct traffic and often provide directions.

Shopping – refer to questions #6 to #12

Dos and Don'ts:

DO try to cut the price down to 1/3 of the asking price in most stores and markets .

DO check the region code on DVDs before you purchase them.

DO NOT buy DVDs or CDs on the street.

DO NOT go with a street solicitor to a DVD store or an alley.

1)Purchasing an item

When you go to a shopping center or a market place, it is not uncommon for two to five salespersons to surround you and to keep pushing you to buy a product. Don't be overwhelmed. It is best to say "Xiexie. Wo buyao." ("Thank you. I don't want it.") in this situation so that they will not bother you anymore.

Xiu Shui Market (aka Silk Alley or Silk Market) and Hong Qiao Market (aka Red Bridge Market or Pearl Market) in Beijing are the top two popular markets for Westerners. The former is more well-known for silk products and Western brand name clothes, such as Ralph Lauren. The latter is more well-known for pearls, arts and crafts, and paintings. While you cannot bargain in every mall or store, you really need to bargain hard in these two markets. You may bargain down to as much as 1/3 of the price initially offered. Sometimes it may be easier to get a better price without a Chinese friend. The reason is fairly simple: Chinese vendors do not like to see their own people help foreigners, who, in these vendors' eyes, have "fat wallets". In addition, the sales clerks at these two markets can be very impolite and rude if you keep bargaining without buying. It is best to only bargain if you intend to buy an item. Furthermore, be aware that many hi-tech gadgets in these markets can sound like a great deal, but might not give you the quality that you desire. For example, digital cameras, camcorders, or iPods may have name brands, but may really be cheap knockoffs.

When you join a tour group, the tour guide will always take you to at least one or two stores. The products, such as jade and paintings, are not necessarily better than the ones you see in other stores, but the prices are usually marked up and could be 15 to 30 times higher than those offered in other stores. Therefore, it would be wise to either bargain hard or to continue shopping around. I would not recommend that you ask your tour guide which item to buy, because a tour guide generally worries more about his or her commission instead of the best deal for you. The highest commission is for arts and paintings, which can be as high as 60% of the selling price. Commissions for jewelry and pearls are normally around 30%.

Almost all Chinese stores refuse to accept a customer's return of their purchase for money or a full refund. The best that a store can do is to replace or exchange a customer's purchase. It would be good to ask about a store's return/ exchange policy before purchasing an expensive item. When you do want to return or exchange a purchase, it is best to go to the counter where you purchased it. If the sales clerk says that the item cannot be returned, then it will not be necessary to talk to a manager, as everyone follows the same policy and a manager does not have the authority to be more flexible when it comes to a rigid no-return policy.

One thing worth mentioning is that beginning in June 2008, Beijing implemented a new rule in which all supermarkets, such as Wal-Mart, will no longer provide plastic bags free of charge. Each plastic bag used is an additional 30 cents (RMB) and customers will be asked whether or not they would like to have one. Most locals now bring their own bag when shopping in order to avoid the additional charge. This does not apply to clothing stores or shopping malls though.

(2) Buying CDs/DVDs

It is true that piracy is still a big problem in China. As you may have heard, pirated CDs or DVDs can be as cheap as 5 *Yuan* (RMB) per disc. However, the Chinese government has doubled its effort to crack down on pirated materials. You may see public notices on bulletin boards, stating that selling or buying pirated CDs or DVDs is a crime and that offenders will be arrested and sentenced to jail. Therefore, you should simply say "no" and walk away if someone tries to sell you DVDs or CDs on the street. Sometimes you will encounter a very friendly middle-aged woman or an innocent teenager on the street who will ask you whether you would like to go to a good store or a place to buy DVDs and CDs. Do not go with any of them. The solicitor is normally a member of a

Judy Zhu

group that sells pirated DVDs and CDs out of a back alley or a rental place.

If you go to shopping malls or department stores, you will be told that all DVDs or CDs are legitimate and that there will not be any problems taking them back to America. Regardless of whether they are actually pirated or not, it is important to be aware that you might not be able to play them on your home DVD players. Generally a region code is encoded with video discs to restrict the regions in which they can be played. The only exception is the discs without a region code. These discs are called all region or region 0 discs.

All commercial DVD players require a region code to play a disc sold in that particular region. DVDs sold in Hong Kong, Macau and Taiwan use the region 3 code, with Hong Kong and mainland China sharing region 6. Region 0 is playable in almost all regions, so it is widely used by China, Hong Kong, Macau, and Taiwan. North America uses the region 1 code, while Australia, Central and South America use the region 4 code. Therefore, it is important to carefully check the region code on the back of the DVDs before you purchase them. On the other hand, it is sometimes possible to region unlock your DVD players. You might want to search on the web for your model if you are interested in knowing more about it.

Dinning out and social gatherings – refer to questions #13 to #37

Dos and Don'ts:

DO bring fruit or health care products when having dinner with a local Chinese family.

DO tap your fingertips lightly on the table after the host or another guest pours you tea.

DO Place the tea pot lid upside down and leave a little opening if the tea pot is empty.

DO NOT turn a whole fish over when dining with Chinese.

DO NOT stick your chopsticks straight up and down into your rice while you talk or drink.

DO NOT wear all-black or all-white attire when going to a Chinese wedding.

(1) General knowledge about dining out with friends

Chinese always order family style meals unless they go to a buffet or a Western restaurant. A family style meal refers to having a number of dishes that everyone is going to share. Traditionally, Chinese fight over who should pay the bill when they finish a nice meal together. Therefore, if you are visiting an old Chinese colleague or friend, you might never be allowed to pay the bill unless you push the issue.

It is common for the person who initiated and organized the diner to pay the bill. On the other hand, Chinese people's attitudes toward Westerners, especially Americans, are deeply-rooted. Americans are generally considered to be wealthy regardless of the current economic recession. In view of this, paying for the meal would show your friendliness and generosity.

More often than not, Chinese people tend to insist on paying the bill while they actually do not want to pay it. The rule of thumb is to give the person opportunity to insist at least three times. If the person still actively insists and has taken money out of his or her wallet, then you should assume that the person really means it. Do not ask "Are you sure?" when a Chinese person offers to pay for the meal, because this sounds like you are happy and want to accept it without trying to offer a similar nice gesture first, which is a normal practice in Chinese culture.

One thing worth mentioning is that more and more young professionals prefer to "go Dutch" nowadays, so in some situations splitting the bill may be appropriate.

(2) Going to a birthday party or a family dinner

Most Chinese birthday parties simply consist of a big lunch or dinner with many gifts from the attendees. In Chinese people's eyes, a good gift is one that shows generosity and care. Therefore, although the emotional value is important, the price you pay for the gift matters to the person who receives it too, because the price and the gift indicate how important the gift-receiver is. This is very unlike what some people in the US believe: "It's the thought that counts." That is why most of the Chinese will leave the price tag attached when giving a gift. That is also why it is always best to bring a gift worth at least 100 *Yuan*, which is equivalent to about $15. It is not uncommon for a Chinese to spend 200 to1,000 *Yuan*, which is equivalent to $30 to $150, when buying a birthday gift for a family member or a close friend. On the other hand, it is not a common practice for Chinese to ask another person what kind of gift he or she wants. In doing so, the effort to get a thoughtful gift, which is much valued, is lost.

When invited to have dinner with a local family, it is best to bring fruit or something healthy, such as fish oil or tea. A bottle of wine could be acceptable, but would seem to be cheap unless it is an expensive brand name foreign wine that values at least 100 *yuan,* which is equivalent to about $15. Bringing a prepared dish or food is not practiced in China.

Whether at a birthday party or a family dinner, there could be people who do not know each other. In these situations, older people are introduced before younger ones, and women before men. When being introduced to someone that is much older, it is polite and common to ask about his or her health by saying "*Nin shenti hao ma?*" ("How is your health?").

Eating in China can be challenging, due to the culture, food and customs. Accepting what the host or your Chinese friends put in your bowl symbolizes, more or less, the acceptance of the Chinese culture and people. Trying as many new things as possible with a pleasant attitude will help you make more friends as well as to keep your host happy. If you really don't want to eat certain foods, then tell the host or your friends that you are allergic to it, so they will still have their pride instead of feeling offended or insulted by a perceived rejection of their fine food.

New Year's Eve dinner is considered a family affair – a reunion of all family members. You should dress formally and nicely if you are invited for this very special occasion. It is also best to bring some expensive out-of-season fruit or health care products.

(3)Eating at a restaurant

When invited by your Chinese friends or business acquaintances to dine at a Chinese restaurant, be aware of the appropriate dress and etiquette. Chinese always emphasize the importance of the group instead of the individual. It will, one way or the other, help you make friends or reinforce friendship if you dress like the majority. In other words, avoid showing your individualism. Rather, it is better to blend in as much as possible. For example, jeans are generally good for all occasions except business dinners. However, if it is a formal dinner and you know that most of the people there will wear a suit or dress, it will be best to follow suit.

When you arrive at a restaurant, you will have to wait to be seated if it is a higher end establishment, such as a

Judy Zhu

restaurant in a 5-star hotel or those that have security guards and hosts standing outside. The security guards working for hotels or restaurants are most likely men. They normally wear uniforms with a red armband. Hosts are generally young beautiful women who wear traditional Chinese *qipao* (a tight-fitting one-piece Chinese dress for women) and stand at the door to greet guests. You might also see a doorman if there is no host. For a family restaurant on the street, you may need to seat yourself.

When ordering food, no particular order is followed unless you are dining in a 5-star hotel that is used to dealing with Westerners. It is very common for people to order six to ten entrees for even just three to four people, because the host wants to make sure that everyone is well-fed. If there is any food leftover after the meal, then the host will be very happy in that he or she believes that the guests are full and have been well-fed. Therefore, do not try to finish the last portion of the dish if you are doing it simply because you do not want to waste any food. Otherwise, the host may end up placing a new order of the dish thinking that you truly like it and that it was not enough. Also, Chinese normally do not take doggie bags home unless only family members or very close friends are dining together. It is a matter of "saving face" in front of their guests and has nothing to do with their wealth.

While higher end or 5-star-level restaurants are more particular about the order in which food is served, most family style restaurants do not follow any specific order when they bring food to a table – basically, whatever is ready is served first.

Dining with your Chinese friends can be very interesting, yet adventurous. Food is generally placed in the center of the table so that everyone can help themselves. The host or other people may place special delicacies on your plate by using their own chopsticks and this behavior is not considered rude – it means they see you as a family member. If you ask them to use a pair of serving chopsticks or a serving spoon, they might take offense, believing that you think that they have poor hygiene. To an uninitiated American the communal pot into which all dip their chopsticks can be quite horrific. Fortunately, with the opening-up and reform policy that was implemented in late 1970s, more and more Chinese have been exposed to Western culture. Many people, especially young professionals, have more awareness of the hygiene issue and cultural differences. Many restaurants, especially those that often entertain Western tourists, have the practice of using a serving spoon. Therefore, most dishes come with a serving spoon or a set of chopsticks, if not, you may request them. At very formal banquets, the servers will serve all courses to each guest, including the hosts.

Although rice is the main staple food for Southern Chinese and noodles or steamed buns are the major staple food for Northern Chinese, most Chinese eat rice with vegetable or meat dishes. When eating, the rice bowl is placed right in front of you or slightly on the left. Rice is eaten with chopsticks after the rice bowl is brought as near as possible to your mouth. As for noodles, they normally are eaten by bringing the bowl to your mouth and slurping them from the chopsticks.

The soup bowl is often put on the right. At some restaurants servers will not put a plate under the soup bowl. Chinese "drink" their soup instead of "eating" it. By saying that, you are supposed to lift your soup bowl and drink directly from it. You may also use a Chinese soup spoon if provided. Chinese soup spoons are wider and shorter than a typical Western soup spoon. After you finish the soup, you may put the spoon in the bowl and put it aside.

Judy Zhu

At an informal dinner, slurping sounds are not only acceptable, but also show that you appreciate the taste of the noodles or soup. It is flattering for the host. However, at formal settings, like a business banquet, this might be considered poor manners.

The names of Chinese dishes on a menu can be very intimidating and bizarre, such as "Hot Braised Lion's Head" and "Sliced Couple's Lungs." These are simply literal word-for-word translations. The former is actually a giant meatball and the later is a famous Sichuan dish that was invented by a couple in Chengdu, Sichuan Province in the 1930's. The dish originally was spicy sliced lungs from cows (at that time the cost of lungs was a lot lower). Later, it evolved into sliced beef. In short, the name of a dish should not scare you away from trying it, just like the name "Bloody Mary" should not scare Chinese from trying the popular Western cocktail. However, do ask about the dish's ingredients and ask how it is prepared before you order it, especially if you are allergic to certain foods.

You might also be offered donkey meat, dog meat, snake meat, boiled fish head soup, uncooked sea urchins, sea slugs, duck blood, monkey brains or a dark green "thousand-year-old" egg, which is made by preserving duck, chicken or quail eggs in mixture of clay, ash, salt, lime, and rice straw for several weeks to several months. The list of exotic foods can go on and on. As strange and disgusting as a dish may sound to you, it would be wise to keep in mind that your host is giving you the food that they like, or food that they consider special. If you reject it abruptly or frown, you might be considered to be rejecting the Chinese culture and hurt the pride of the host. Therefore, do not reject their food unless you really have to. At least, give it a try.

Another thing that is popular on the table which requires a lot of knowledge to eat properly is a whole-fish dish, such as "Steamed Fish" or breaded "Sweet and Sour Fish". No matter how the dish is cooked, it is always served whole with the head and tail still attached. The head of the fish points to the guest of honor when it is served. The guest of honor will be asked to use his or her chopsticks to divide the fish. The word for fish, "*Yu*", is a homonym of the word of abundance. It symbolizes prosperity and wealth. Turning the fish over is a taboo, because it signifies bad luck - the fisherman's boat capsized, so your wealth is gone. Fish bones are supposed to be put on the table unless a special plate is provided.

As for table manners, you should put your chopsticks flat on the table or on the chopstick rest if provided when you do not want to hold them in your hand. Never stick your chopsticks into your rice while you talk or drink, because for Chinese, especially the older generations who are superstitious, this signifies bad luck and a death in the family.

Never try to lift and balance your food by holding one stick in each hand. Using your sticks as a spear or fork is also considered inappropriate. You may use your hand for certain foods, such as chicken feet, ribs, a whole crab, or shrimp that still has the tail attached.

Tap the fingertips of your right index finger, middle finger, and ring finger at the same time lightly on the table to indicate "thank you" when your host or the person next to you pours you tea.

You should not belch or burp at the table. As mentioned earlier, slurping is fine unless it is at a business banquet. Be aware that a lot of Chinese chew food without closing their mouths. Unlike Americans who swallow their food before speaking, Chinese often speak with food still in their mouth.

When you need more drinks, you will need to place another order, sometimes even for tea. It is worth noting that most Chinese restaurants in China do not provide complimentary tea. Rather, they have a tea menu from which you can order, including healthy and popular varieties, such as barley tea, Chrysanthemum tea, and eight treasure tea. Chinese find adding sugar and cream to tea very strange. On the other hand, some people do use rock sugar for Chrysanthemum tea and the Eight Treasure Tea. To signal the server for more tea, place the tea pot lid upside down, or open it if it is attached.

If you are a non-smoker and are often bothered by second-hand smoke, you may want to go to higher end restaurants since most of them have both smoking and non-smoking areas. If you end up dining in a family style restaurant, please be prepared to see or even bear with the fact that many Chinese there may be smoking. Trying to stop a Chinese from smoking would be considered rude. Chinese smokers believe that smoking, no matter where they are, is their legitimate right. Most Chinese are not aware of how annoying it can be.

You might notice that many Chinese people talk really loudly in public. Please do not jump to the conclusion that they are rude or lack consideration for others. From a linguistic point of view, Chinese, as one of the most widely studied tonal languages, uses pitch to signal a difference in meaning between words. These pitch variations are an important part of the language, just as stress and proper word order are in any language. In the Chinese language, word meanings or grammatical categories are dependent on pitch level, such as tense. Therefore, it is not unusual that Chinese use a higher pitch than English speakers, and as such, they are considered loud or even annoying in public. Nonetheless, at a restaurant it will be considered rude if you ask a Chinese to lower their voice, unless you are very close friends or there are some sensitive matters concerned.

When you want to call a server, try not to hiss or snap your fingers, especially at higher end restaurants. Doing so is considered poor manners, but generally will not insult a server. To signal them, you must try to catch eye contact with him or her. Simply say "*fuwuyuan*." ("Excuse me, server.") About ten years ago, customers used "*xiao jie*" ("Miss") or "*xian sheng*" ("Mr.") to address servers. However, with the evolvement of language and subtle new connotations of the words, "*fuwuyuan*" is much more appreciated than "*xiao jie*" since "*xiao jie*" has become slang for the word "prostitute."

When you are finished eating, lay your chopsticks down on your chopstick rest or neatly place them on the table to indicate that you are done. Orange slices, watermelon chunks, or other pieces of fruit might be served at the end of the meal to help cleanse your palate. However, the main purpose is to keep you healthy. In China the importance of eating fruit after a dinner can not be overemphasized. In fact, Chinese do not eat desert or drink coffee after a meal. However, with the quick spread of Starbucks and many Western coffee shops in major cities in China, coffee is getting more and more popular among young professionals. It is considered cool and trendy to socialize with friends at a coffee shop.

When you want the server to bring you the check, you may simply say "*mai dan*", which means "check please." American traveler checks, personal checks, or credit cards are generally not accepted unless you go to a five-star hotel. Tips are not necessary for any restaurant on the mainland unless you are in Hong Kong, where tipping is more common.

It is wise to have enough cash with you if you plan to pay, because your American debit card will not be accepted. However, if you are a guest, or if you dine with an old-fashioned Chinese, you will not be allowed to pay no matter how hard you try, though you should still insist on paying at least a couple of times. Please do not tell your host that he or she does not have to pay and that you do not mind buying, as this sounds negative in Chinese. The connotation is that you are forced to buy due to the circumstance. The best thing to do is to say *"Xiexie"* ("Thanks") again and again. It would also be appreciated if you tell them how much you enjoyed the food and if you offer to treat your friends or acquaintances the next time you dine together. For example, you could say, *"Zhen hao chi. Duo xie le. Xia ci wo qingke"*, which means "It tastes great. Thank you so much. Next time will be my treat."

(4) Tipping

Chinese people value a sense of personal worth and their contribution to others. Good service is given to foreigners without any expectation of receiving a tip. In Chinese eyes, poor service to foreigners would cause a loss of face for their employer or even their country. Therefore, your unexpected tip will be rejected even if you insist that they take it. On the other hand, most 3-star to 5-star hotels in China automatically add a 10-15% service charge for your lodging. You pay what you see on the bill and that is it. It's worth noting that some service personnel in hotels and restaurants that cater primarily to a Western clientele are more likely to expect tips, so are English speaking tour guides who generally expect 20 to 50 *Yuan* tip from each Westerner, which is about $3 to $10.

(5) Drinking and Toasting

First and foremost, keep in mind that you should not drink tap water, because it has not been purified. If you would like to have some water at a restaurant, ask for bottled mineral water or hot tea.

At a party or get-together, Chinese men normally drink a lot and will ask all guests to drink along with them. If you do not drink anything at all, you will be considered unfriendly. As the Chinese saying goes, *"Jiu Feng Zhiji Qianbei shao."* ("Even a thousand glasses of wine is not enough when in the company of a good friend.") Drinking and even getting drunk actually shows that you cherish their friendship. However, we do know that drinking too much is not good for our health, so if you do not drink, you may have to explain why or even tell a little white lie. In fact, if you simply tell your Chinese friends that you do not drink at all, more often than not, they will keep pushing you to try. You will be surprised by their persistence. Therefore, it is not a bad idea if you tell your friends something like *"Wo de yisheng bu rang wo hejiu."* ("My doctor does not allow me to drink.") or *"Duibuqi, wo dui jiu guomin."* ("I am allergic to it.") In doing so, non-drinkers will happily avoid any frustrating situations involving drinking.

Toasting is a very important part of Chinese dinners and banquets. A well-suited toast can lighten the atmosphere and help make new friends quickly. Therefore, the rule of thumb is making sure that the toast you are giving is appropriate to the intended audience and occasion. It is always wise to express your appreciation to the host and others for the wonderful food and the great opportunity to experience the Chinese culture. It is also a good idea to have two or three short toasts memorized for when the opportunity presents itself. For example, for a senior friend's birthday party, you may say *"Zhu nin fu ru dong hai, shou bi nan shan."* ("Wish your happiness is as endless as the East Sea and your longevity is as the South Mountain.") or *"Ganbei."* ("Bottoms up.")

Ganbei literally means "dry glass", and has the connotation that people should drain a glass in one swig. However, this likely applies to *"baijiu"* more than any other type of drink. *Baijiu* is distilled liquor that usually has 50 to 65% alcohol content, and is generally made from rice, sorghum, or other grains. *Maotai*, made in Guizhou Province, is China's most famous brand of liquor. Beijing brewed *Erguotou* is a very famous brand as well, but is much cheaper. Since a shot glass is used for *baijiu*, it is more doable to *ganbei* ("bottoms up"), especially if you can hold a lot of liquor.

Beer is very common in China and is served in nearly every restaurant. Chinese people take pride in their local products, so most of them like to order the most famous local brand. For example, in Beijing people will order Beijing beer or *Yanjing* beer. In Qingdao, people will order Tsingtao beer. You may be surprised that Budweiser is considered the No. 1 American beer by most of the Chinese and Blue Ribbon is quite popular too. This has a lot to do with commercials and marketing.

It's important to know that most places serve beer at room temperature, regardless of the season, though places that cater to tourists might serve it cold. Therefore, if you want it cold, you will need to tell a server.

Red wine is also common in China. Anyone used to European, Australian, or American wines will likely be surprised by the taste of Chinese wine, which is much sweeter. Great Wall, Dynasty, and Chang Yu are all well-known brands. Chinese people take a lot of pride in them, even though they consider drinking imported wine as more upscale and trendy.

Chinese people are also very enthusiastic about various medicinal liquors, which usually contain herbs and/or animal parts. Some of these include ingredients like ginseng, while others contain some unusual ingredients, such as snake blood. These liquors are generally very expensive.

Regardless of whether it is red wine, white wine, or rice liquor, you normally have to order a bottle or more, because

Chinese restaurants do not sell wine or liquor by the glass or liter.

(6) Night market

There are a lot of night markets in China. Beijing, for example, has a famous night market called Donghuamen Night Market, which is located west of Wangfujing Avenue, the biggest and the most modern shopping area in Beijing. This noisy and bustling market is open every night and is great fun to visit. All kinds of Chinese food are available there, such as pot stickers, BBQ, noodles, cumin mutton on sticks, even BBQ scorpions and roasted snakes. Dozens of food stalls are arranged next to each other with a great variety of food. All of the stalls in the Donghuamen Night Market list their price on a white board on top of the stall or in front of the stall. The price of food items can be bargained for, especially when purchasing multiple items.

Although this type of market is managed by the local government and food inspections are frequent, you still need to be very careful when choosing food from these vendors if you have a sensitive stomach, especially if you want something cold. Many Chinese believe that a little liquor will help to kill the germs if you eat some food like BBQ scorpion. However, it is not clear whether this is based on scientific research or personal anecdotes.

(7) Bars

There are many Western style bars in major cities like Shanghai, Guangzhou, and Beijing. Two well-known and popular bar streets in Beijing are Sanlitun and Houhai. The former has been around longer, while the latter is relatively new but becoming more popular. The reason is that the Houhai area is behind Beihai Park and has a beautiful view of the lake. Unlike in the United States, you do not need to show any form of ID in order to get in a bar or order alcohol in China, because there is no legal age limit for people who want to consume alcohol as long as they are adults. According to the Chinese Constitution and other laws, one is considered to be an adult when turning 18.

There are often young and beautiful women in the bars. They might be patrons, trying to relax and enjoy the night life, or they might be "Miss Promotion" waiting to play drinking games to get you to consume more. Once in a while, there might be underground prostitutes depending on which bar you go to. Therefore, although you can hit on someone at a bar, you have to be aware of what you want and whom you are dealing with. Also be aware of what they might think you want. In addition, as a foreigner, plenty of girls will hit on you. Since Chinese people generally believe that a proper girl will not go to a bar, especially by herself, you might want to be careful with a girl who is there alone and tries to hit on you.

Chinese are generally not very open to homosexuals. Therefore, trying to strike up a conversation with the same sex is acceptable, but hitting on or flirting with the same sex may not be accepted in mainland China. Hong Kong is more open to this though.

In discos and fancy bars with entertainment, you will notice that the price of imported beer is about 40 *Yuan* to 50 *Yuan*, which is about $6-7.

As in restaurants, tipping is not expected. As a matter of fact, tips can be insulting for a bartender since tipping is not practiced in China and can be considered a condescending gesture.

(8) Invitations

Unless there is an occasion like a wedding reception or business banquet, Chinese people do not send formal written invitations by mail. Emails, phone calls, and direct face-to-face verbal communication are the most common forms of invitation. You are expected to RSVP at your earliest convenience, regardless of how the invitation is sent. If you cannot make it, give the host a good reason so there will not be any misunderstandings or hard feelings caused by your absence.

When you do receive a formal written invitation for an official function or big event, such as a business banquet or a wedding reception, the proper way to RSVP is still by phone or email.

(9) Weddings

When going to a Chinese wedding reception, do not wear all-black or all-white attire, both of which are associated with death and mourning.

Red envelopes with over 1, 000 *Yuan* cash, which is about $150, are the favored gift and are becoming more popular as the cost of weddings rise. People like to choose lucky numbers for the amount of cash that will be given, such as 1, 888 *Yuan*, because "8" resembles fortune and wealth. This has something to do with the pronunciation for the number 8, which is "*ba*". "*Ba*" sounds like "*fa*," which means making a fortune. Many Chinese will do whatever it takes to get a phone number with as many "8s" as possible, and some people will even pay extra to have it in a license plate.

At some point toward the end of the reception, the bride and groom will walk around to each table and toast the guests. This is the time that you can toast them and take pictures with them.

After the wedding, do not expect a thank-you note for your attendance or gift. This does not mean that they are not appreciative. Chinese generally do not follow this practice unless they have been educated in the West and have incorporated it into their own lives.

Transportation and travel – refer to questions #38 to #47

Dos and Don'ts:

DO expect to see and use squat toilets.

DO take tissues when traveling.

DO ask the taxi driver to give you a receipt.

DO carry cash in a money belt or other secure places.

DO NOT take a "taxi" that does not have a taxi sign.

(1) Transportation in general

Many people, both Chinese and foreigners, travel by train for long distance trips. It is one of the cheapest ways to travel in China, and all train stations are always very packed. Therefore, you should pay extra attention to your belongings and be watchful of any thieves.

Also, bear in mind that the Chinese train system was designed for the local population to be economical and efficient. Most Westerners find the conditions on trains, such as the seating, bathrooms, and dining facilities, to leave much to be desired. Generally speaking, the "soft sleeper" offers the most comfort for long trips, and bathrooms can include Western sit-down toilets as well as the Eastern squat toilets. Shortly after boarding, an attendant will come to your compartment to collect your train ticket and give you a travel card that has your berth number. Before the train arrives at the destination, the attendant will take back the travel card and return your train ticket. Unfortunately, many of the staff working on the train do not speak any English.

When you walk out of the train station, you may encounter some Chinese who want to trade their "hard seat" train ticket for your "soft sleeper" ticket. This could be for higher expense reimbursement from the company that they work for. Since you do not need a train ticket to exit a train station, you can trade it or give it away if you do not want to keep it as a souvenir.

In Hong Kong, cars are driven on the left side of the road, but the rest of China drives on the right side. However, driving in China is not recommended for those who are not experienced. First of all, though many countries recognize an American driver's license, China does not, nor does it recognize an international driver's license provided by the American Automotive Association (AAA). Therefore, you will not be able to rent a car or a motorcycle in China unless you have a Chinese driver's license. Secondly, traffic in the big cities can be quite chaotic – you will encounter many traffic jams, rush hour or not. Taking public transportation, especially the subway, is often more economical and efficient. Last but not least, Chinese drivers have their own unspoken driving rules – it looks extremely chaotic for outsiders, but is very orderly amongst themselves. For example, it is not uncommon for people to cut in with full speed without using any turn signals or to disregard pedestrians crossing the street.

Taking a taxi is not complicated in China. You may go to any Taxi stop which normally has a big "taxi" sign in both Chinese (出租) and English, along with a picture of a cab. Or you can simply stand by the side of the road and wave at any taxi that is passing by. All taxi drivers are supposed to use a meter and will give you a receipt after you pay. Keep the receipt, because if you want to file a complaint or contact the driver for a lost item in the cab, it will make it easier. It is always wise to carry a card with the name and address of the hotel where you are staying so that you can get back to the hotel if needed. Tipping is not necessary even if it is a long distance drive.

Meanwhile, you may see some cars without taxi signs parked outside a scenic spot, offering people taxi service. These are illegal taxis and should be avoided. The Chinese government has been making great efforts to crack down on the so-called "black car". However, due to the lack of public transportation in some areas, there are many such "taxis" in the suburbs. Do not use this type of "taxi" service, because they can rip you off or cause some other unexpected problems for you.

Public transportation has seen huge improvements over the past few decades, especially in big cities like Beijing and Shanghai. A special transportation debit card, known as "*Yi ka tong*", can be purchased at any subway station and at most bus terminals. One can simply swipe his/her card when getting on a bus or going through a subway entrance to pay the fair. Cards are very inexpensive, convenient, easy to use, and can be purchased in different denominations.

Most of the buses and all of the subways have recorded stop announcements in both Chinese and English. You may see both Chinese characters and English letters on a big screen as well. The newest subway in Beijing, line 8, was designed solely for the 2008 Beijing Olympics.

China is known as the kingdom of bicycles. Bicycles are one of the major means of transportation for working people. Thus, it is not surprising that roads are swarmed with hundreds and thousands of bicyclists trying to make their way to and from work or school every day. You can easily rent a bike in most cities. Some rental places require a photo ID (your American driver's license may work depending on the store) and a deposit, while others require just a deposit. You have to be very skilled at riding bikes, because there aren't any designated bicycle lanes in China. Consequently, cars and bikes mingle together. When people cut in, no matter whether they are driving a car or riding a bike, it can be very dangerous. Therefore, think twice before you decide to use a bicycle as a means of transportation in China. Also, surprisingly enough, Chinese people, drivers or passengers, do not wear helmets, because they are not required to do so, nor are they accustomed to the practice.

(2) Taking pictures

Chinese people like to have pictures of themselves. Therefore, it might be surprising for Westerners to see many Chinese, young or old, pose in various scenic spots, or even just in front of a wall or a gate. Meanwhile, many people, especially those who are from a small town, take pride in having a picture of themselves taken with a Westerner. It is not uncommon for Westerners to be asked to be in a photo with some Chinese they do not know. This is simply a gesture of friendliness and admiration of Western culture. Unfortunately, you cannot expect them to send you the pictures through email or mail.

At the same time, please be advised that street names and scenic spots are sometimes written in both Chinese and English. Keep in mind that some of the English translations might be misspelled or even grammatically incorrect. This is because they were translated by Chinese who simply used a dictionary as their only resource. Many Westerners find these translations so funny that they want to take a picture of them. It is not prohibited to do so, however, some Chinese can be very humiliated by this behavior. Therefore, do exercise caution and think twice before you take these types of pictures.

(3) Bathrooms

In the big cities of China, you may see some of the world's finest restaurants and most modern hotels, all of which have excellent toilet and bath facilities – including "Western Style" toilets. Even on the street or at parks, there are more and more public bathrooms available compared to ten years ago. A few of them still charge a nominal fee for use, but many of them are free. In some public bathrooms, especially those at airports, or big shopping malls, you will also see people working in the bathrooms, constantly cleaning the already clean sinks or mopping the floors. They are full-time workers and tipping is not necessary.

However, in rural areas or older buildings, you are likely to encounter "Eastern style" squat toilets. Some of these are extremely smelly and dirty. In addition, toilet paper, paper towels, or sinks are often not available. Squat toilets come in different forms - a hole in the ground or a shiny porcelain fixture with "footprints" flanking the aperture. In any case, do bring toilet paper and hand sanitizer with you when you go to these bathrooms. If you find using a squat toilet difficult or annoying, just console yourself with the knowledge that many Chinese find sit-down toilets non-hygienic and inconvenient to use.

Although many of the public bathrooms nowadays are equipped with toilet paper, paper towels and hand dryers, it is always wise to take hand sanitizer and paper with you when you travel. This is because sometimes the toilet paper is placed in the very front of the bathrooms and you will not realize that the stall is not equipped with toilet paper until it is too late. Also, some bathrooms are not well attended and can simply run out of toilet paper over the course of the day.

(4) Traveling in the countryside

Traveling through the countryside in China can be arduous as the unpaved roads can be quite dirty and public bathrooms are sparse. Even if you do find a bathroom, the filthiness can be beyond your imagination. In addition, people there generally do not speak any foreign languages. They rarely see foreigners and might stare at you long enough to make you feel uncomfortable. They are simply curious about you and will not do you any harm.

When traveling through the countryside, you might encounter some friendly farmers who give you a fresh tomato or a juicy cucumber. Do not eat them right away, because they are often not well-washed. Thank them and tell them that you will eat it later. To be safe, if you go to a countryside restaurant, order something that is hot and well-cooked, such as noodle soup, so that you can avoid any raw or uncooked meat or vegetables.

It is wise to carry some contact information for medical facilities with you while you travel in the countryside. It is also wise to take with you all prescription and nonprescription medication you may need in your carry-on bag.

Names – refer to questions #48 & #49

Dos and Don'ts:

DO address the parents of your friends as "Shushu" (uncle) and "Ayi" (aunt) if your friends are about the same age as you.

DO NOT assume that a married couple has the same family name.

DO NOT address people by their first names.

Chinese usually carry a clan surname, which is always placed first. This is followed by one or two characters which represent the first name. Unlike the west, Chinese do not use middle names. Women do not change their last names when they get married, although they did in the old days. When a couple has a child, they often ask the grandparents or a specialist to give the child a good meaningful name. Nowadays some people are more liberal and a child can carry the mother's surname, though it is still quite rare. The reasons for taking a mother's surname can be various. For example, a woman is more financially secure and is a firm believer of feminism. Or the man acquiesces to the wife's wishes. It may also have something to do with social status or the meaning of the couple's surnames.

Many people from Hong Kong and Taiwan were educated at missionary schools and have a Christian first name, which comes before any of the others – as in John Ma Yueming, which should be called Mr. Ma, or to his English speaking friends, John Ma.

The way Chinese people address one another denotes their relationship, social rank, or status. For example, only family members and spouses might use a person's first name to show the kinship and intimacy. Colleagues, friends, and sometimes couples, address a person by calling his or her full name with the family name first. A mistake can be an outright insult or can make a person very uncomfortable. So can switching to a given name without the other person's permission. Generally speaking, it is safe to stick to the following courtesy rule when addressing Chinese: (1) Family name + professional title; (2) Family name + first name + salutation (such as "Mr." or "Ms"). For example:

(1) Zhang Zong Jingli: Zhang – family name, *Zong Jingli* – professional title (General Manager)

*(2) Zhang Lifu Xiansheng: Zhan*g – family name; *Lifu* – first name; *Xiansheng* – salutaton (Mr.)

Addressing the father and mother of your friends as "*Shushu*" (uncle) and "*Ayi*" (aunt) shows the notion of being a family and being close. However, if you are too close in age to your friend's parents or even older than they are, you should not use these two terms. Rather, you may simply say "*ni hao*".

Customs and social practices – refer to questions #50 to #68

<u>**Dos and Don'ts:**</u>

DO bring gifts when you have dinner with a local family at their place.

DO be prepared to see a price tag when receiving a gift from a Chinese friend.

DO be prepared that Chinese see KFC and McDonalds as high end Western food chains.

DO be prepared for questions regarding your age, salary and the cost of your car or house.

DO NOT give white flowers as a gift.

DO NOT give a clock as a gift to an older person.

DO NOT give a green hat as a gift to a man.

DO NOT talk about sex in general or anyone's sex life.

DO NOT respond with a "thank you" when being complimented.

(1) Important traditional Chinese holidays

The Chinese New Year, which normally occurs in late January or early February, is one of the most important festivals for Chinese across the world and is determined by the lunar calendar. During the 15-day long celebration, people get together with family and visit their friends and relatives. Shops are nicely decorated, with red and gold being the typical lucky colors of the Chinese New Year. Temple fairs are popular, as are fireworks. Children are given lucky money in a red envelope by their parents and relatives to ward off evil spirits. Since many people go back to their hometowns to visit their family, train stations are often extremely packed.

The Lantern Festival is the 15th day of the first month of the lunar year. Beautiful red lantern exhibits, lion and dragon dances, and eating "*Tang Yuan*" (ball-shaped boiled sweet rice dumplings with stuffing, such as red bean paste and black sesame paste) are the typical features of this festival. It also marks the end of the Chinese New Year celebration.

Qing Ming Day is on April 4th (or April 5th when there are 29 days in February) and is also known as "Tomb-sweeping Day". This is an occasion for Chinese to visit the graves of their ancestors. Many people, especially those who follow traditions, could travel across the country to tidy up the tombs of their departed.

Duan Wu Festival is also called Dragon Boat Festival. It takes place on the 5th day of the 5th month of the lunar year. It is said to be celebrated in memory of *Qu Yuan*, a famous patriotic poet of the then State of Chu during the Warring States period (475-221 B.C.). He drowned himself in protest because his emperor gave in to the bully State of Qin. The people of Chu worried that fish might eat his body, so they launched their boats and started to throw "*Zongzi*" (sticky rice dumplings with dates or meat as stuffing which are wrapped in bamboo leaves in a pyramid shape) into the river. The people also beat drums to scare away any fish. To symbolize the attempted rescue of *Qu Yuan*, Chinese race narrow long boats made of wood (the front of the boats are carved into a dragon's head, therefore the name) to the beating of a drum. In addition, eating *Zongzi* is a well-preserved tradition.

Mid-Autumn Festival is on the 15th day of the 8th month of the lunar year, which is normally in mid September of the calendar year. It is second only to Chinese New Year in importance and is similar in significance to an American Thanksgiving. On this day, people get together with all of their extended family members. At this time, the moon is the fullest and largest of the year. Children are told that on the moon there is a fairy living in a cold crystal palace with her sole companion being a rabbit. A heavenly general and friend would occasionally pay her a visit, bringing along his special wine, which would make her dance gracefully. Children watch the shadows on the moon and find the story fascinating. Eating a big family dinner and enjoying the full moon are the typical features for this festival. Moon cake is a must for this celebration. People like to buy fancy and delicious moon cakes as gifts for family, friends, and even colleagues.

The National Celebration Day is on October 1st. It is also the anniversary of the founding of the People's Republic of China in 1949. Grand parades occur during the day and fireworks and official parties with performances occur in the evening. Chinese government employees enjoy three paid days-off. During this long break many people travel out of town to visit their family or simply tour around. Therefore, the train stations are as packed as during the Chinese New Year.

(2) Giving and receiving gifts

Giving gifts in China can be a very challenging experience. A proper gift is expected and should be given if you wish to start or continue good "*guanxi*" (connections). Chinese people usually prefer practical, useful, or fancy items that are factory-produced instead of those that are hand-made or home-made. IPods and other hi-tech gadgets can be good gifts for younger people. Ginseng candy or Ginseng tea is a popular gift from Americans for older people. The root of ginseng is the basis of traditional Chinese herbal medicine and is believed to possess a wide variety of therapeutic properties. North American ginseng in particular has been rated top quality and is thus considered a valued gift in China. Meanwhile, local or international health products are always appreciated by Chinese, such as *Pu'er* tea, fish oil, or even multivitamins. If you know that your host drinks or smokes, famous-brand name cigarettes or liquor can be good gifts as well. Imported chocolates or toys are considered good gifts for any children of the host family. In addition, any brand name items with international, national, or local prestige can be good gifts as well.

Do not give a bouquet of white flowers as a gift, because it is a symbol of mourning. Do not give a clock to Chinese, especially an older person, no matter how fancy or expensive it is. This is because the Chinese word for clock, "*Zhong*", is a homonym of the words for termination and end. Therefore, for many Chinese, a clock is a symbol of termination of life. Another taboo gift is a green hat for a man. This is very insulting for a Chinese man because of its cultural connotation. "*Gei ni dai lu maozi*" is slang and can literally be translated into "give you a green hat" or "give you a green hat to wear". The real message is "your woman is having an affair".

When you choose wrapping paper, red and gold are popular colors that symbolize happiness and fortune. They are best for wrapping a new year's gift or a wedding gift. As for gifts for other occasions, any wrapping paper can be fine except for black and white paper, because those colors symbolize mourning.

When receiving a gift, Chinese normally do not open it until they get home, because they want to share it with their family. Although years ago, almost everyone would not open their gifts right away, nowadays it is not uncommon to see some young people open them immediately. Being eager to see the gift, being less conservative about their feelings, and the influence of Western culture, have all contributed to this change.

Be aware that removing the price tag from a gift is not widely practiced in China. Many people keep the price tag with the gift to show the monetary value of the item, especially when the item is expensive. This is because Chinese people generally want to let the gift-receiver know how much they spent on the item. Many jewelry or arts and crafts have a very high price tag, but people can pay much less when purchasing them. This has something to do with the marketing and selling technique which makes customers believe that they are getting a good deal. In addition, customers might feel that such an item can be a decent and presentable gift.

Chinese also tend to regift and do not consider the behavior inappropriate. Some people will even tell you this honestly. For example, a Chinese can give a very expensive international brand name tie to a friend, and tell the friend it is actually a gift from a business associate. The behavior stems from the belief that being willing to give the valuable away means that they value you and would like to share with you as they do with their family. You are expected to feel warm and treasured instead of being insulted.

(3) Asking for and returning favors

Chinese like to help their friends because they believe that one can not survive without a family and that friends are part of that family. They also believe that family should always be there for each other. Reciprocation is important in order to keep lasting and good relations with one another. Treating friends to a nice meal is a common practice when trying to return a favor, as is purchasing a nice gift for the friend or the family members of the friend. Both McDonalds and KFC are considered high-end Western food chains in China. Even Papa John's is very popular - fancy decor, expensive pizza, and trendy Chinese crowds often amaze Americans going there for their first time.

When you want to ask for a favor, the word "*qing*", the Chinese equivalent of "please" sounds very demanding to Chinese. Therefore, try to say "*ke bu keyi mafan n*i....?" which can be translated into "May I trouble you to...?"

(4) Karaoke

If you go to Karaoke with Chinese people, you should be prepared to sing songs, whether it is in Chinese or English. You may not be able to get out of it by saying that you are off-key or that you do not like to sing. What matters to Chinese is your team spirit and willingness to be part of the group. Some Chinese can even be very pushy in this situation. Elvis as well as country songs are popular in China, thus if you sing any of these songs, it will be much appreciated. Of course, a popular Chinese song will be even better.

(5) Punctuality

Chinese are generally very punctual. If you have a dinner appointment with a Chinese friend at 6: 30 p.m., then it is safe to be there at 6: 25 p.m. to get ready for the dinner. The rule of thumb is that the host should be 5-10 minutes early and the guest can be 5 minutes early or right on time. On the other hand, if you haven't seen or heard from your friend by 7: 00 p.m., do not leave or simply eat by yourself unless you are told so in advance by your friend. The best thing to do is to drink some tea and wait for another 30 minutes. Traffic can cause people to be quite late in the big cities. Therefore, calling your friend and leaving a message is acceptable, but calling the friend's spouse or other friends may seem like an overreaction. When socializing, some Chinese people use the term "Asian-time" to refer to being an hour late from the stated time of arrival. It is not considered rude or late since the gathering is not formal.

(6) *Receiving and presenting business cards*

The formal way to present and receive a business card is to use both hands. Putting a name card in your pocket right away can be considered rude. Most Chinese would expect you to take a good look at the card that is given and then to address the person with the right status title or salutation such as "Mr." or "Ms." If you do not have a name card holder in your briefcase, you may put it into your wallet.

(7) *Conversational topics*

You might be surprised that Chinese people often ask questions about private information. Talking about age, regardless of gender, is quite common. Asking about salary or even the price for a private car or residence is also very common. Therefore, expecting Chinese to ask personal questions will prepare you to be friendly instead of being offended.

On the other hand, Chinese generally do not talk about sex or their own sex life. It is considered a non-public, "dirty" topic. Talking about other people's sex life is taboo as well, and it can make listeners very uncomfortable.

(8) *Praise and criticism*

Do compliment Chinese, but expect them to decline and say something like "*Nali nali,*" which means "I am so flattered" or "not really". It is a long held traditional belief that one should always be humble. If someone compliments you, you should show humility by politely declining. For example, do not say "*Xiexie*" ("Thank you"), rather, say "*Nali nali.*"

Chinese in general can take constructive criticism very well due to the lasting belief that one can only make progress when he or she is given criticism, especially constructive criticism. As the Chinese saying goes, "*Liangyao ku kou liyu bing, zhongyan ni er liyu xing.*" This can be translated into "Good medicine can treat and benefit you, although bitter to the mouth; earnest advice/criticism can help you grow, although unpleasant to the ear."

(9) Elderly

In China, the elderly are considered wise and to have a lot to offer. Showing great respect to and for older people is demanded everywhere in China. For example, Chinese people believe that parents' advice should be followed.

When entering or exiting a facility, the elderly are always asked to go before the younger ones. Also, all people on a bus are expected to give their seat to seniors as soon as they get on. When trying to give your seat to an elderly person, it is best to tell the ticket conductor first so that the ticket conductor can announce that the seat is available for the elderly person and to make sure that he or she can walk to the seat on the packed bus. You can also let the elderly person know if you are next to him or her.

Seniors enjoy a lot of special benefits in China. For example, starting in 2009 Beijing seniors who are above 65 can ride all public transportation for free. Admission to all community parks is also free.

Chinese people often address an elderly female as "*Dama,*" "*Ayi,*" or "*Nainai,*" which mean "great aunt," "aunt," and "grandma," respectively. An elderly male can be addressed as "*Shushu,*" "*Dashu,*" or "*Yeye,*" which are equivalent to "uncle," "big uncle," and "grandpa," respectively. This applies to many situations, including when they meet for the first time or if they are strangers on the street.

(10) Theaters and concerts

If you are a man and ask a Chinese woman (or a woman asks a Chinese man) to go to a movie with you, more often than not, it will be considered a date. At least it is a sign of personal interest unless you have been good friends for a while and have been hanging out a lot. Most men will pay for the movie tickets and snacks when they go to a movie with a woman. Unfortunately, most Chinese ladies will not thank the man for paying for the dinner or movie, because it is expected and it is a custom.

There are some movie theaters that will assign a seat number on your ticket which you are supposed to use to seat yourself accordingly. It is not common for a person to ask his or her neighbor to switch seats.

When watching a movie with your friend, it is not considered rude to ask questions with a lower voice. As a matter of fact, you might hear other Chinese whisper something as well. If you watch a movie with a date, it is expected that the man will show affection by holding the woman's hands or by kissing her occasionally. In fact, many theaters have private booths for couples. However, some older Chinese are not comfortable showing affection in a theater. Moreover, they tend to have negative impressions of those who do show affection.

When Chinese go to theaters or concerts they do not consider a little chatting to be a rude behavior. People might ask questions and share opinions, but will try to speak with lower voices so that they do not disturb their neighbors. In addition, for concerts or shows, you may applaud at any time that you feel is appropriate (normally when the majority of the audience applauds). Sometimes you might see the speaker or performer clap at the same time that the audience applauds; it simply means "Thank you" and "mutual positive feelings" instead of being improper or immodest.

(11) Sneezing

If you sneeze, many Chinese will first worry whether you have got a cold. If not, a Chinese will tell you "someone is missing you." If you keep sneezing, your close friend might say "someone is cursing you." Those phrases are widely used and the phrase "bless you" is not embraced by the Chinese.

Some American students say "*Yibai sui*" ("100 years old") after a Chinese sneezes, but this sounds very strange to a Chinese who will actually say something like "*You ren xiang ni.*" ("someone is missing you.") if you sneeze once. If you keep sneezing, a Chinese will tease you by saying "*You ren ma ni.*" ("Someone is cursing you.") Simply put, the English phrase "bless you" can not be translated literally under this circumstance, because Chinese people simply have a different approach.

(12) Living with parents

Living with one's parents is a common occurrence in China. People who are over 30 or over 40 years old may still live with their parents, if both sides are okay with it. Many Chinese find paying rent while living in their parents' house foreign and strange. Although they do not pay rent or utilities, most of them do buy groceries or other items for the household. In Chinese eyes, parents are family forever and family members do not need to pay each other. Some couples even live with their parents because of the convenience – retired parents will cook dinner for them and will help take care of any children.

On the other hand, Chinese either move into their parents' house or let the parents move in with them when the parents get older. They believe that being caring and giving is the ultimate goal in a family. They make sure that their parents get loving care from family members. It is hard for many Chinese to understand why many Western elderly stay at a nursing home.

Hand gestures and body language – refer to question #69

<u>Dos and Don'ts:</u>

DO remember the connotation of patting one's own stomach.

DO NOT point your index finger directly at someone.

DO NOT cross your arms when talking.

In China the middle finger does not mean the same thing as it does in America. As a matter of fact, it does not have any connotations at all. However, pointing the second finger directly at someone is considered rude. It often means blaming the person whom you are talking to or that you have a lack of basic social manners.

Touching or pointing to the tip of one's own nose with a raised forefinger is quite common. To Westerners, the gesture would seem slightly funny. To Chinese, it simply means "It's me" or "I'm the one."

One or both hands lightly patting one's own stomach means "I am full". It is not uncommon to see this kind of body language at the dinner table.

Crossing your arms while you are talking is generally considered arrogant or condescending.

Street phenomenon – refer to questions #70 to #78

<u>Dos and Don'ts:</u>

DO be prepared to see people smoke, spit, and litter on the street.

DO NOT make the assumption that two women who are holding hands on the street are homosexuals.

DO NOT give cash to any beggars.

(1) Physical contact

Westerners are often shocked or surprised by the hand-holding or arm-holding behavior between two women or sometimes even three women. This is simply a sign of friendship and does not have any sexual connotations. It is important to know that although the younger generation can be more expressive than the older ones, Chinese people are generally very reserved and do not show affection in public. It is not uncommon to see old men walk several paces ahead of their wives, but this does not necessarily suggest that they are not a happily-married couple. The reason is very simple. Traditionally, a man was the head of a family. A woman was supposed to be submissive to her husband and to follow her husband's lead in all matters.

(2) Fights or abuse

Street fighting is not a common occurrence in China, but it does happen. Sometimes a very small thing can cause two angry people to get into a big fight. Try to walk away instead of asking what happened. If you can find a security guard nearby, the best approach is to report the problem to them and let them handle it. If it is a very serious fight, and you see some injuries or it appears life-threatening, call 110 or ask someone else to call the number if you do not have a cell phone.

Once in a while you might see some unpleasant situations. For example, an angry woman kicks a man on the street or a man keeps spanking a child. You might consider it abuse and want to intervene or call the police. Please think twice before taking any action. It will not be a surprise for a Chinese to learn that the angry woman who kicks the man simply is showing her unhappiness with her boyfriend or husband. They might be smiling at each other and laughing at her drastic behavior minutes later. The man who spanks a child on the street might simply want to discipline his child. Parents' spanking a naughty child is not uncommon in China and it is completely acceptable.

(3) Beggars

There are rich and poor people everywhere around the world. However, there are also many organized, professional beggar groups in China, especially in big cities like Beijing and Shanghai. When you give money to these professionals, who can be old women in thin shabby clothes, or even unfortunate handicapped children, you'll get a swarm of them in just a few seconds. These people, especially the heads of these organizations, dine at high-end restaurants and buy expensive goods at shopping malls after getting money from kind-hearted people.

It is reported by the Chinese print media that only around 15% of the beggars are truly poor and need help. To crack down on professional beggars, the Chinese government encourages people to call the police if they think someone is in dire need of help. This might not be practical for foreign students or tourists to handle this type of issue because of the language barrier. Therefore, giving beggars some food when they ask for money might be more feasible, yet kind enough. In doing so, hungry people get the help they need. Meanwhile, you do not have to worry about being scammed or helping bad people do wrong things, such as buying drugs or alcohol.

(4) Smoking and littering

Smoking is considered not only good for social interactions, but also cool and trendy. It is very common to see people smoke on the street – whether waiting for a bus or simply out for a walk. As annoying as it can be, the best thing you can do is to pass them by quickly and forget about it.

Littering is still a big problem in China. Although there are various trash cans on the streets or in parks, especially in bigger cities, people are often seen littering anything from cigarette butts to plastic bags and bottles. There is no fine for littering and it is a common practice in many places around China.

(5) Spitting and nose-blowing

As disgusting as it might be, spitting or blowing one's nose in public without the use of a handkerchief or tissue paper is fairly common in rural China. People who are raised in this kind of environment tend to consider this type of behavior acceptable. When these people move to big cities, they bring their habits with them. That is why sometimes you see this in the city and even in restaurants.

With the ease of transportation, people often travel from place to place. In view of the globalization and China's image in the world, the Chinese government is redoubling its effort to reduce spitting in the cities, but it still happens in many public places. Most city people see this kind of behavior as a sign of "low" class or lack of education. Once in a while, it happens that children go to the bathroom in public. This behavior annoys even the locals, but normally no one takes any action to prevent it.

Safety and medical treatment – refer to questions #79 & #80

Dos and Don'ts:

DO always guard your wallet or purse.

DO always carry with you a list of important numbers and contacts.

DO always have some cash with you for purchasing food or items.

It is reported that China has one of the lowest per capita crime rates in the world. Guns are strictly controlled and you rarely hear about shootings or robberies. If you are in a downtown area or some commercial districts of a big city, it is generally safe to walk on the streets at night, even after midnight. Many shops remain open until 10:00 p.m. or later and there are plenty of street lights. However, you have to exercise caution if you are in the countryside or a suburb, because it is normally very dark and there are not many people around. If you get lost or something happens, it will be very hard to reach someone for help.

No matter where you are, Westerners are normally not the target of crime, because offenders get a more severe penalty if the crime involves foreigners. This affects China's image to the world, so the Chinese government tries all means possible to raise people's awareness. In addition, if a crime involves a foreigner, many media, especially foreign media, will inevitably report about it and will follow up on the case. This is the last thing that the Chinese government or an average Chinese person wants to happen.

As in any big city, pick-pocketing is quite common in such cities as Beijing, Shanghai, and Xi'an. It is important to guard your wallet or purse no matter whether you are out shopping, taking public transportation or are out touring around. Never put your bag at your feet while checking schedules or lose sight of it.

Con artists are not uncommon in cities that are flooded with tourists. They favor tourists as they are easy targets. You might be approached on the street and offered a better rate to exchange your US dollars into local currency, or you might be offered a free gift at a particular store that they want to take you to. You will be fine and safe as long as you refuse them politely instead of making a deal with them.

Knowing how to use public phones and learning some key phrases in Chinese might be helpful if you encounter something unexpected. I would encourage you to always carry with you phone numbers and addresses of the US Embassy or consulate and other important places like foreign clinics. Keep a photo copy of your passport and ID stored in a hotel safe while you carry your original documents.

Depending on where you go and what you want to do, you may need to carry cash from time to time. Many stores or restaurants do not accept checks or credit cards, so having cash is important if you plan to dine out or to purchase many goods. It is a good idea to constantly check your pocketbook when you are in a crowded area. Even in a restaurant, make sure that you have put your money in a safe place from which no one can snatch it. Men's wallets are best in a sealed pocket in the inner side of a jacket. Lacking that, the front pants pocket will do too, or even a concealed money belt. Be alert if someone jostles you in a crowd, because he or she might be distracting you while an accomplice attempts to pick your pocket.

If you suspect that you have any serious medical or dental problems, you may check with the US Embassy or consulate and ask for advice before going to see a doctor. If you cannot reach anyone there, feel free to go to a local hospital. The medical facilities in big cities like Beijing and Shanghai are comprehensive and impressive. You just need a guide or a friend to tell you which one is the best for you. Please note that in China hospitals require immediate payment for any diagnostic services or medical treatment. A list of English-speaking medical facilities in major cities in China is provided in Appendix IV. If you get sick in a rural area, it will be more challenging, because there aren't many medical facilities. In addition, it will be harder to find a clinic that has medical staff who speaks English. The best thing to do is to take precautions and have a Chinese friend or a tour guide travel with you. Carrying with you some medications that you frequently take will be helpful too.

Conclusion

In spite of the need I see to have a reference book on modern Chinese Cultural Encounters, I realize that there is always more material than I can cover in one book. Therefore, Volume I only focuses on studying and traveling in China. More in depth discussions will follow in Volumes II and III, which will focus on working and living in China, and doing business in China, respectively.

Although there are some similarities between the American and Chinese cultures, there are also many distinct features and unique aspects to each. Traveling with an open mind and being prepared for new experiences will help you to successfully deal with various cultural encounters, thereby allowing you to enjoy your Chinese study or trip to China.

APPENDIX I

COMMON CHINESE GREETINGS AND USEFUL PHRASES

Number	Chinese	English
1	Ni hao!	Hi
2	Ni hao ma?	How are you?
3	Hen hao.	Very good.
4	Xie xie.	Thank you.
5	Duo xie.	Thanks.
6	Bu yong xie.	My pleasure.
7	Bu keqi	You are welcome.
8	Duibuqi	I am sorry.
9	Mei guanxi.	It's ok.
10	Lao jia.	Excuse me.
11	Qing.	Please.
12	Mei wenti.	No problem.
13	Xing.	Ok (to agree).
14	Xie xie. Wo buyao.	Thank you. I don't want it.
15	Qing wen, ce suo zai nar?	May I ask where the bathroom is?
16	Wo bao le.	I am full.
17	Hao chi.	It's tasty.
18	Nali nali.	I am so flattered.
19	Wo bu dong.	I don't understand.
20	Zai jian.	Good-bye.

APPENDIX II

Important Phone Numbers in China

1. Ambulance: 120

2. Fire: 119

3. Police: 110

4. Traffic accidents: 122

5. Weather: 121

6. Time: 117

7. Local directory: 114

8. International operator: 115

APPENDIX III

Important Holidays in China

January 1	New Year's Day
The 1st day of the 1st month of the lunar year	Spring Festival (The Chinese New Year)
The 15th day of the 1st month of the lunar year	Lantern Festival
March 8	International Women's Day
April 1	Tree-Planting Day
April 5 (or April 4th on a year with February 29th)	Qing Ming (National Tomb-sweeping Day)
May 1	International Labor Day
May 4	Youth Day
The 5th day of the 5th month of the lunar year	Duan Wu (Dragon Boat) Festival
June 1	International Children's Day
July 1	The Chinese Communist Party's Birthday
August 1	Army's Birthday
The 7th day of the seventh month of the lunar year	Chinese Valentine's Day
The 15th day of the eighth month of the lunar year	Mid-Autumn Festival
September 10	Teacher's Day
The 9th day of the 9th month of the lunar year	Chongyang Festival (Senior's Day)
October 1	National Day

APPENDIX IV

English-speaking Medical Centers in Major Cities in China

Beijing: (area code 10)

1. **Beijing Asia Emergency Assistance Clinic (AEA)**
   Suite 105, Wing 1, Kunsha Building, No 16
   Xin*yuan*li, Chaoyang District
   Tel: 6462-9100 or 6462-9112

2. **Beijing International SOS Assistance (SOS)**
   Suite 105, Wing 1, Kunsha Building, No 16
   Xin*yuan*li, Chaoyang District
   Tel: 6500-3419 or 6500-3388

3. **Beijing- International SOS Clinic**
   Suite 105, Wing 1, Kunsha Building, No 16
   Xin*yuan*li, Chaoyang District
   Tel: 6462-9117

4. **Beijing Toronto International Hospital**
   No 1, Ronghua Rd (M), Developing Zone
   Tel: 6554-1728

5. **Beijing United Family Clinic – Shunyi**
   Pinnacle Plaza, Unit 818, Tian Zhu Real Estate
   Development Zone, Shunyi District

Tel: 6433-3960
Emergency Number: 6433-2345
Website: www.unitedfamilyhospitals.com

6. **Beijing United Family Hospital & Clinics**
#2 Jiangtai Lu, Chaoyang District
Tel: 6433-3960
Emergency Number: 6433-2345
Website: www.unitedfamilyhospitals.com

7. **Beijing United Family Health & Wellness Center – Jianguomen**
#21 Jianguomenwai Dajie (B1, The St. Regis
Residence, St. Regis Hotel), Chaoyang District
Tel: 8532-1221
Emergency Number: (86-10) 6433-2345
Website: www.unitedfamilyhospitals.com

Guangzhou (area code 20)

1. **#1 Affiliated Hospital of Guangdong Medical University**
1 Yangjiang Road
Tel: 8333-7750 ext.3046
Emergency hotline 8333-6797

2. **#1 People's Hospital (Global DoctorClinic)**
1 Panfu Road
Emergency Hotline 8108-0509, 8333-6797
Mobile 135-7003-5254
Email: guangzhou@globaldoctor.com

3. **Can Am International Medical Center**
5F Garden Tower, Garden Hotel, 368 Huanshi
Dong Lu
Tel: 8386-6988

4. **Guangzhou Children's Hospital**
   318 Remnin Central Road
   Emergency hotline 8188-6332 ext.5103

5. **Guangzhou International SOS Clinic**
   Room 152, Dongshan Plaza, 69 Xian Lie Zhong
   Road
   Tel: 8732-6253

Haikou: (area code 898)

Hainan People's Hospital
#8 Longhua Road
Tel: 6864-2660,6622-3287 (outpatient)
Emergency hotline 6622-5866/6666/2423

Hangzhou: (area code 571)

North American International Hospital
419 He Fang Road, Hang Zhou City
Tel: 8778-0120

Harbin: (area code 451)

1. **Harbin #1 Hospital**
   151 Diduan Street, Daoli District
   Tel: 468-3864, 461-4606, 461-4636

2. **Harbin Medical University #1 Hospital**
   #5 Youzheng Street, Nangnang District
   Tel:364-1918, 360-7924, 364-1563

Hong Kong (area code 852)

1. **Hong Kong Adventist Hospital**
   40 Stubbs Road
   Tel: 2574-6211
   Website: http://www.hkah.org.hk/

2. **Hong Kong International SOS Clinic**
   16/F World Trade Center, 280 Gloucester Road,
   Causeway Bay
   Tel: 2528-9900

Kunming: (area code 871)

1. **First attached Hospital of Kunming Medical University**
   153 Xichang
   Tel: 532-4888
   Emergency hotline 0871-532-4590

2. **Yunnan Provincial Maternal and Child Hospital**
   #20 Gu Lou Road
   517-7000

Nanjing: (area code 25)

1. **International SOS Clinic, Hilton Hotel**
   319 Zhong Shan Road
   Tel: 8480 2842

2. **Jiangsu Provincial People's Hospital**
   300 Guangzhou Road
   Tel: 371-4511

Shanghai (area code 21)

1. **Shanghai - American Medical Center (Global Doctor)**
   4Pangjiang Road, Dadong District
   Tel: 2433-06778/ 2342-6409
   Emergency 2432-6409

2. **Shanghai International Peace Maternity Hospital**
910 Heng Shan Road
Tel: 6407 0434 ext. 1105

3. **Shanghai Dental - DDS Dental Clinics**
- 1) Puxi Clinic
Peregrine Plaza, B1-05, 1325 Middle Huai Hai Road
Tel: 5465-2678 or 5465-5766
- 2) Hong Qiao Clinic
Suite 2, 85 Jin Hui Road
Tel: 3431-7387
- 3) Pudong Clinic
POS Plaza, B1-F, 1600 Century Ave
Tel: 6876-0409 or 6876-0447
24 hr Dental Emergency: 13162001688
Website: http://www.ddsdentalcare.com

4. **Shanghai East International Medical Center**
551 South Pu Dong Road, Pudong
Tel: 5879-9999

5. **Shanghai First People's Hospital, International Medical Care Center**
585 Jiu Long Road (near the Bund)
Tel: 6324-3852

6. **Shanghai Huadong Hospital Foreign Clinic**
221 Yanan West Road
Tel: 6248-3180 ext. 3106, 3107

7. **Foreigner's Clinic of Shanghai HuaShan Hospital**
15th Floor, Zong He Lou, 12 Middle Wu Lu Mu Qi Road
Tel: 6248-3986 or 6248-9999 ext. 2531

8. **Shanghai Physical Therapy & Pain Management Clinics**
   Rm 601, Shanghai Center,1376 West Nan Jing Road
   Tel: 6279-8920

9. **Shanghai Children's Medical Center**
   678 Dongfang Road , Pudong District
   Tel: 5873-2020

10. **Shanghai United Family Hospital and Clinics**
    - 1) **Changning Clinic**
    1139 Xian Xia Road
    Tel: 5133-1900
    24 Hour Emergency hotline: 5133-1999
    SHUPtservice@ufh.com.cn

    - 2) **Minhang Clinic – SRC Clinic**
    Shanghai Racquet Club, Ground Floor Clubhouse,
    Lane 555, Jinfeng Lu, Huacao Town
    Tel:2201-0995
    24 Hour Emergency Hotline: 5133-1999
    srcclinic@ufh.com.cn
    Website:http://www.unitedfamilyhospitals.com

11. **Shanghai World Link Medical Centre**
    Room 203, West Tower, Shanghai Centre (Portman
    Hotel), 1376 Nanjing Xi Lu
    Tel: 6279-7688

12. **Xujiahui New Pioneer International Medical Centre (NPIMC)**
    2/F, Geru Building, 910 Hengshan Lu, Xujiahui.
    Tel: 6407-0434

Shenyang: (area code 24)

Liaoning Province People's Hospital
#33 Wenyi Road, Shenhe District
Tel: 2481-0136, 2414-7900

Shenzhen: (area code 755)

Shekou International SOS Clinic
Ground Floor, CMIT Building, No. 9 Industrial
Road South Shekou
Tel: 2669-3667

Suzhou: (area code 512)

1. **Suzhou No. 2 People's Hospital**
    26 Dao Qian Road
    Tel: 523-3141

2. **Suzhou No.4 People's Hospital**
    16 Bai Ta Xi Road
    Tel: 727-3853

3. **Second Affiliated Hospital of Suzhou Medical College**
    181 San Xiang Road
    Tel: 828-1647

Xi'an: (area code 29)

Xi Jing Hospital
No. 17 West Changle Road
Tel: 337-5548 (foreigner service section) or 337-4114 (operator)

APPENDIX V

TO-DO LIST IN PREPARING FOR YOUR TRIP TO CHINA

Preparation checklist:

1. Book an air ticket through a travel agency at least one month ahead of time.

2. Confirm your reservation of the air ticket and your seat numbers with the airlines.

3. Visit the airlines' website to get information for air travel to China, such as security requirements and rules and regulations.

4. Apply for a passport or make sure that your passport is valid for at least the next six months. Otherwise, you will not be eligible to apply for a visa, nor will you be allowed to board.

5. Apply for a visa by using a travel agency. This normally takes between five to ten days. You may also go to a nearby Chinese consulate in person and get a visa on the same day if you pay a $30 rush service. Information about procedures and required documents can be found at http://www.china-embassy. org/eng/hzqz/zgqz/t84246.htm.

6. Schedule an appointment with your doctor 6-8 weeks before traveling to get a Hepatitis A vaccination and other recommended shots, such as tetanus.

7. Make hotel reservations and airport pickup service if needed.

8. Book a tour through a hotel or a travel agency.

9. Check what your insurance covers and buy travel insurance if needed.

10. Familiarize yourself with customs procedures and requirements.

11. Make copies of your important documents, such as passport and hotel information.

12. Shop for gifts if you are going to visit Chinese friends.

13. Make arrangements for paying bills, holding mail, house-sitting, etc.

Packing:

1. Check the weather forecast online and pack enough suitable clothes.

2. Put all original documents in your purse or your bag that you will carry with you at all times. An extra copy of each document should also be packed in a carry-on suitcase.

3. Pack medication that you need or might need, such as aspirin and Imodium.

4. Pack all gifts that you have prepared.

5. Put cash and credit cards in a safe place and keep the credit card customer service number in a separate place for emergencies.

6. Put a list of contact numbers in your purse or a safe and accessible place.

APPENDIX VI

RECOMMENDED ONLINE RESOURCES

1. CHINA BRIEFING
 http://www.uschina.org/info/china-briefing-book/

2. AREAS IN CHINA OPEN TO FOREIGN
TRAVELERS
http://www.usembassy-china.org.cn/us-citizen/opencity.htm

3. TRAVEL CHINA GUIDE
http://www.travelchinaguide.com/essential/safety.htm

4. TRAVEL TO CHINA
http://www.cnto.org/aboutchina.asp

5. TRAVEL TO CHINA
http://www.lonelyplanet.com/china

6. APPLYING FOR A VISA ONLINE
http://chinavisaservice.org/application.asp

7. APPLYING FOR A VISA AT CHINESE EMBASSY OR
CONSULATE
http://www.china-embassy.org/eng/hzqz/zgqz/t84246.htm

REFERENCES

Althen, G (1988). *American ways.* Yarmouth, ME: Intercultural Press..

Avery, Peter and Susan Ehrlich (1992). *Teaching American English Pronunciation*, Oxford: Oxford University Press.

Axtell, Roger (1993). *Do's and Taboos around the World. 3rd Edition.* New York: John Wiley & Sons.

Bosrock, M. Mary (1997). *Put Your Best Foot Forward Asia.* St. Paul, MN: International Education Systems.

Chaney, Lillian & Martin, Jeanette (2000). *Intercultural Business Communication.* 2nd Edition. Upper Saddle River, NJ: Prentice Hall.

Crystal, David (1991). *A Dictionary of Linguistics and Phonetics*, Cambridge, MA: Basil Blackwell.

Ford, Charlotte (2001). *21St – Century Etiquette.* Guilford, CT: The Lyons Press.

Mesthrie, R., J. Swann, A. Deumert and W. Leap (2000). *Introducing Sociolinguistics.* Philadelphia, PA: John Benjamins Publishing.

Singer, M. R. *The role of culture and perception in communication. In Weaver, G.R.(Ed), culture, communication and conflict: readings in intercultural relations.* Upper Saddle River, NJ: Simon & Schuster.

Wanning, Esther (2003).   *Culture Shock*. Portland, OR: Graphic Arts Center Publishing.

THE AUTHOR

Professor Judy Zhu, a Beijing native who resides and works in Monterey, California, is a member of the Chinese Language Teachers Association of California (CLTAC) as well as a member of California Writers Club (CWC). In addition to her education in teaching a foreign language, she also earned a Master's degree of Conference Interpretation from the Graduate School of Translation and Interpretation at MIIS, an Affiliate of Middlebury College.

Professor Judy Zhu, whose pen names include Jasmine, Shuishan and Suxin, began publishing her works at the age of 14. At the age of 15, she won Third Place at the International Chinese Poetry Contest and her poem *Speechless Winter* was published in the book *International High School Chinese Poets*. At the age of 17, six of her essays were included in the five-volume series of *Beijing Top Ten High School Award-winning Writings*. Before she came to the US for graduate school, she had won many literature awards in China and her 300 plus poems, prose and stories were published in national newspapers and magazines as well as being broadcast by national radio stations in China. She was also an invited part-time columnist for *Teda Times* when she worked in Beijing.

More information about her can be found at www.chinese-consultant.com.